TORQUAY
TORNADO

Published by
Lubin Publishing
4 Stokecliffe House,
114 Park Road,
Bristol BS16 1DT
www.zerolubin.org

First published 2012

ISBN: 978-0-9563077-1-2

Designed and produced by Louise Burston

Woodcuts for Parts 1-4: Ben Goodman
Illustration of boxing gloves on title page: Alex Green

Front cover design: Alex Green
www.mstrgringo.com

Front flap: *Meadfoot Beach, Torquay, Devon*
Back flap: *Torquay, South Devon, by night*
Copyright John Hinde Ltd/John Hinde Collection
www.johnhindecollection.com

Printed by
HSW Print
Tonypandy
South Wales

TORQUAY TORNADO
PAUL KING
A MEMOIR

ADAPTED FROM THE ORIGINAL MANUSCRIPT BY

STEVE CHAMBERS

Lubin Publishing
www.zerolubin.org

DEDICATED TO PETE BRYEN

Dear Gerry,

The book was born when I was introduced to your Dad in the Dolphin pub, St Marychurch, Torquay. When he heard I was a journalist he got quite excited and said I should write his life story.

Later that week I met him again and he produced a brown dog-eared scrapbook - obviously treasured. The fact he trusted me to borrow it was, I felt, not only a great compliment but also a reason to read it - as a favour.

Later that evening I made a pot of coffee and began to read. By 4am and loads of coffee later I'd read it about six times and just knew I had to follow it up.

We used to meet at his house in the morning and talk about his life. This was difficult because he would often go off on tangents but gradually I managed to bring the pieces together to complete a remarkable story.

Paul always said he loved the end result of my efforts that made everything worthwhile. The days we spent together were extremely special, we had so much fun and laughed all the time. Gerry, your Dad was such a very special person. His passing left life less colourful.

Pete

PETE BRYEN

ACKNOWLEDGEMENTS

Many thanks to all those who have made the publication of this book possible and for everyone out there whose continuing help, support and encouragement keep Zero Lubin going the distance.

With a special mention to Pete and Lyn Bryen, Steve Chambers, Brian and Edna Yeatman, John and Jackie Povey, Atila Mustafa, Tim Bouquet, Patrick Wray, Vasanta Suddock, Pauline Newton, Georgia Cockerell, Sophie Pettifor, Chris Broughton, Ian George, Bill at Central Books, Will Self, Stewart Home, Jeremy Howell and David Duke.

Fairground photographs on pages 41, 46-47, 52, 54, courtesy of the National Fairground Archive, University of Sheffield Library

Photograph of Newton Abbot Butter Market, page 29, courtesy of Newton Abbot Town & GWR Museum.

Photograph of Paul and Gerry King, page 226, courtesy of Vivienne Genaway.

CONTENTS

PART FOUR: FINAL ROUNDS

THE BEST OF THE REST BY GERRY KING

GLOSSARY OF BOXING TERMS

'In real life a person is an unknowable jumble of contradictory qualities. Brave and cowardly. Cruel and kind. Treacherous and loyal. Feckless and prudent. In fiction this would be confusing ... This is a mistake writers of biography make. They try to shape a life, to give it a fictional coherence. They should tip the whole lot on the page and say:

"Here is a life of sorts. Make of it what you will".

Willie Donaldson, *The Henry Root Letters*

★ PAUL KING

GLOBAL ID	**30845**
BIRTHDATE	**1931/08/07**
DEATHDATE	**2010/04/21**
DIVISION	**Welterweight**
COUNTRY	**UK**
BIRTH PLACE	**Dumfries, Scotland, UK**
RESIDENCE	**Torquay, Devon, UK**

TOTAL FIGHTS **59**

Won 33 (Knockout 13)

Lost 19 (Knockout 6)

Drawn 7

Rounds Boxed 387

PART ONE

THE RICH SMELL OF LEATHER

KITCHEN SPARRING
THE RICH SMELL OF LEATHER
THE APOLLO
A GOOD SHOW
LIFE ON THE BOOTHS

TORBAY

May your Ship ⁕   ⁕
Sail out on Sunny Seas
⁕ Starry Nights ⁕ ⁕
and a favouring breeze
⁕ May any clouds ⁕
that come your way
Be Silver lined ⁕ ⁕
⁕   and blow away

TORQUAY

Queen of The English Riviera
in Glorious South Devon

CHAPTER 1

KITCHEN SPARRING

Right from the very beginning I had a first class education when it came to avoiding punches. I would be standing in the kitchen or sat in the lounge when suddenly my mother would hook me round the head. Mystified and in pain I would demand a reason and invariably she would give me one, 'for giving Granny cheek last week; Mrs Bath saw you eating chips in the street out of a paper bag; that jumper was clean when you put it on'. She was an unpredictable boxer, my mother; she'd drift up noiselessly like a gas attack and descend from behind, or launch herself upon me as I came in through the door. She'd swing either fist, left or right or both together, with equal weight and timing, and always with unimpeachable confidence and composure. I could have cowered and taken it, but to act like that was never much in my nature.

When someone is bigger than you are, speed is your first recourse and she forced me to move. After a while I could skip and duck or block her untrained flails; I'd see her coming and bob and weave before her arms had even begun to quiver. I learned from the way her veins bulged and created tiny ridges on her forehead that she was going to strike, and soon her only weapon was stealth. I would tire her body long before her will gave in, and then she'd sit on a kitchen chair and berate me with words instead. Of course, at that time I would never have called what I was doing bobbing and weaving, it had no artifice, but was as natural as the way a hare will never run in a straight line when in danger and instead carve a crooked path across the field. Prior to this I had never seen an unusually bulbous glove or a man thrown against a fence of ropes, take a beating and show solidarity to his attacker when it was finally over. Before I had ever tried to understand this strange ritual, I was already being inducted into its rites and my first teacher was my mother.

However, these kitchen sparring sessions aren't my earliest memories of boxing; that accolade I can accord to my father. He had always been seduced by the verve of sport; he was a footballer himself and said he'd had a trial for Torquay United. With him I heard my first punch; in 1937 he kept me up late to keep him company as he listened to the transcontinental radio transmission from Madison Square Gardens of the Joe Louis v Tommy Farr fight. My father told me we were rooting for Farr because he was Welsh. My world was very young in 1937; I knew that Wales was close and America was at an incomprehensible distance, and only this certain knowledge coloured my first boxing match. I simply couldn't understand why a Welshman would ever go all the way to America for a fight. My father's way of aiding my understanding was to tell me that they were fighting for the heavyweight championship of the world, which did nothing but hurt my brain more than any punch ever did.

Though my actual memories of that confused introduction to boxing were less of the sport than of the geographical location: what a fight it was to begin with! It was Louis' first defence of his heavyweight title and Tommy Farr lost only on points to a man who had knocked out fourteen of his previous fifteen opponents and would do the same to fourteen of his next fifteen too. Yet, unable to make a story out of the sounds I heard, it's as though those rhythmic commentary tones and hysterical spectator whoops somehow settled in my subconscious. For when World War II began its upheavals and with one of its mightiest heaves transported Joe Louis across the Atlantic, on a boat this time rather than the airwaves, it unloaded him at Torbay. He boxed an exhibition at Plainmoor and there I met him, still heavyweight champion of the world, which he remained until well after I had tightened my laces for the first time.

Joe Louis (left) and Tommy Farr

I had watched Joe Louis box, but Tommy Farr watched me. Some of his fellow Welshmen from the Glamorgan cadets followed in the American world champion's foot-shuffles and came to box in Torquay against my own army cadet team. We boxed back and won, and the Tonypandy Terror was there to see it all and to present me with the cup afterwards. I have met many famous boxers and most much more intimately than I did the duo whom one night in 1937 had countless cauliflower ears striving intently at their wirelesses, but none when I was so young and when my relation to boxing was nothing more certain than youthful exercise. Whether bad or good, Joe Louis and Tommy Farr were the earliest influences on me and for that I have ever been in their debt.

I wasn't born in Torquay; my family first moved there when I was four. We had a small, two bedroomed flat with an outside toilet. The flat was over a builder's garage at the end of a courtyard. Other flats surrounded this courtyard and when I'd go out to the toilet, although I had no evidence, I always felt the neighbors' spying eyes. Housing a family of four, the flat had exclusive cosiness about it. A Valor oil lamp provided warmth in the winter months and my mother, with the eternal diligence of the house proud, would trim the wick to ward off the paraffin smell. We had no electricity; we were a purely gas powered family, for both cooking and lighting. The wireless that beamed boxing from New York had a battery as its dynamo, and my father would take it to a local electrician to be recharged. In the bedroom I shared with my sister there was a skylight. I would lie on my bed and watch the raindrops put out the stars until it seemed as though I could see a subterranean city and I'd hug my hot water bottle and imagine myself floating on it until I fell asleep.

When World War II was declared in 1939 my father joined up, along with many other boys' fathers. I missed him; this was not unusual. First he was sent to France with the British Expeditionary Force and after he worked as a dispatch rider in the Battle of Britain. Later he was posted to Malaya. At the fall of

Singapore he was captured by the Japanese and had to endure the disdain and brutality inflicted on those who had surrendered. Whilst in captivity he was transferred to help construct what afterwards became known as the 'railway of death' in Burma. Three years and ten months after Singapore, with the Japanese defeated, he was freed, emaciated, suffering from malnutrition and desperately exhausted. But he still had to endure a slow steam across the world's two greatest oceans; tracing an equatorial path along the Pacific, cutting out the Americas with the Panama Canal and then following the Gulf Stream back to Blighty.

At the end of the war it was not unusual to see demobbed soldiers, so when one day I was chatting to my friend Tony in our street and I saw two soldiers approaching from the end of the road, I barely registered their presence. As they came closer I glanced at them again and noticed that the smaller looked Far Eastern. Although British soldiers weren't unusual, Asian ones certainly were. My eyes moved to his companion and it took me a few moments to recognize him. I don't remember what our first greetings were, only the military smell of his khaki uniform as he embraced me. My father was home.

The man who accompanied my father was Chinese, his name was Chang and all his family had been killed in the war. I never really discovered why, but he wanted to begin a new life in England and my father offered him accommodation with us as a platform from which to do it. He stayed for a while, got a job in a launderette and eventually moved to Southend. That was all I ever knew of him. It was a strangely compassionate act from my father, one that underlines my impression of him: that he was always more interested in his mates than in his family. And so it proved when he received his backdated army pay. He spent a few weeks of reunited bliss, meeting up with old chums, marvelling that they were still here and celebrating as men who had fought a war and experienced the fragility of life. Then, after the initial

My Father, Joseph King

My Mother, Joan King

elation, when life shifted into a more familiar gear, it became obvious that the engine was straining.

While my father had been away, my mother had developed a highly wrought way of life: disciplined and habitual. When my father returned there was no place for him in this new orderliness. Eventually they must have come to some sort of mutual, unarticulated agreement because one morning my father sidled up to my bed where I sat reading, discretely handed me a ten shilling note and told me he was going to Canvey Island to visit his elder brother. He told me to be a good boy and look after myself and all the unimaginative things people say when they leave without an explanation and a set date for their return. The house was quiet and he didn't want to disturb the peace, so he shut the door imperceptibly as he left. Not more than ten minutes later I was joined on my bed for a second parental chat of the day. If my father was mysterious, my mother blew the fog away like a sudden hard breeze from the north. She said she had managed to get job in Swindon, but that there was only enough room where she would be staying for one child and that it was better that my sister, Edna, went with her. I would have to go and stay with Aunt Ethel.

That was that. In a single, unexpected day, my home, my family and all that I had been used to had disappeared. As I sat on the bus, bound for the Torquay suburb of St Marychurch, I passed Plainmoor and was reminded of the time I had met Joe Louis there a few years before, but at that moment nothing seemed to matter. It had begun to rain and walking from the bus stop to Aunt Ethel's house I was soaked through. Although my sister and I called Ethel and her husband Sid, Aunt and Uncle, in reality they were just family friends who fostered because they couldn't have children of their own. Ethel, at least, had the experience to deal with abandoned children, but my arrival was unannounced and her surprise was evident. The loss of my home made me vulnerable in a way only a child can experience. From then on I never felt more at home than when wearing a pair of boxing gloves.

Amateur Bouts, Torquay Carnival 1948

CHAPTER 2

THE RICH SMELL OF LEATHER

At the time my family left I was training most nights at the YMCA or a boxing club called the Apollo. My involvement with these clubs began when I was at school. I played the usual team sports that are the foundations of a school's physical education: football and cricket. I enjoyed them immensely and was always eager to participate. Then one day the teachers informed us that we could try boxing if we wanted. They delivered a speech about boxing being character building and that life was hard and we would benefit from the physical fitness and mental endurance.

They didn't need to tell me this; I became involved straight away. There wasn't much instruction but I didn't think I would need any, believing fighting to be instinctual. There was no ring; we boxed on the gym floor lined with worn mats. I was put against a boy who, I quickly found out, had boxed before. I was all aggression and swung out like a closing time thug, giving no thought to defence or movement. The teachers bellowed at me to get my guard up and, again, get my guard up, and again, and that was all they offered me. Having previously only listened to boxing I had no idea how a guard was formed, as jab after jab rocked my head back and jarred my neck. They didn't even tell me to roll with a punch to absorb the shock, never mind how to do it. After a couple of humiliating minutes the boy caught me a powerful shot to the eye socket and the teacher rang the bell with his mouth. "That's it! That's it! King, let someone else have a go." Adding, as though his reasoning was obvious "Get your guard up next time." The only edifying thing about my first bout of boxing was a biology lesson on the development of a black eye.

After that I was set against boxing for a time and it wasn't until I was at a secondary modern school that my antipathy had become diluted enough to pull gloves on once more. My school by this time was Audley Park and the teacher who inspired me was called Mr Powell. It's funny how writing this up now I am able to recall the names of the school and the teacher where boxing was finally explained and an understanding reached, whereas at my previous school I only remember a bleak, ill-equipped gym and well-paid childminders. Finally, after all my brushes with the sport, I was instructed in the basics with simple language and direction. I was taught what a guard was, and how to stand and move and the difference between a jab, a hook, a cross and an uppercut.

I can remember running home and saying to my mother "I want some new boxing shorts, I'm boxing in the school team." That very evening, with great ingenuity, she crafted a pair of smart shorts from my sister Edna's dark blue school knickers. She pulled out the elastic from the bottom of each leg and stitched a strip of white fabric up the sides.

Mr Powell was the first to see something in me and he tentatively told me after one session that he thought I seemed to have some ability and that if I worked at it I would develop my skills and might even be quite good. That encouragement, the small amount of belief that it was, planted aspirations where previously there were none.

Soon my humbleness gave way to arrogance, not overbearing; I was not one to regularly give it voice, but a provision that I knew was necessary for success. Quiet but alive, it was within me, a welcome remedy to aimlessness. There has never been a pursuit that arrogance is more suited to than boxing, which is not all beauty of skill and form but anticipation and spectacle too and the most like a story of any sport, it abounds with nicknames and caricatures. A sport defined by a peerless moment; a single drop or thrust or fall of connection. A moment that if missed, and so easily is it missed, remains inexplicable. Only television cameras, absent from much of boxing's history, can rectify this; the recording played again and again, not for pleasure or wonder, but for understanding; the understanding of a primal, yet illicit, urge. However, even if there was nothing mysterious for boxers about such a moment and even though we were full of arrogance, I was still scared to shaking before each bout.

I remember the extreme strangeness of boxing at the beginning. The rich smell of leather in your face, the feeling of vulnerability as you stand there in shorts and vest; the thought that violence was to be committed towards you. When you first start, because you are unused to it, your eyes water from the shock of a blow landing on your face, especially if you are hit in the nose, then gradually you become inured. But it is only your physical reactions that learn to accept the frequency of trauma; the psychological tension is always wound up. Yet some fighters are like one I knew, Terry Downes, who upstairs was a steel mill, built on heat and duress. His arrogance was of the blasé type, as though he just didn't care about pain. His style was beyond intricate tactics and functioned to a single tenet: to hit harder than he was hit, because he knew he'd get hit, but he thought it as regular as breakfast. However, Terry was an extreme example. Most fighters, like most people, have an aversion to getting hurt. If in a boxing match you have to dictate the motion of a fight, to establish hegemony over it and make the other man work for you, first you had to find a way of overcoming the tremble and the fright.

With Terry, it was as though he allowed his opponent free speech and then berated him in the confidence that his own voice would be louder and stronger. Other fighters would try to silence their opponent, repressing the right of the other man to allow his fists a say. My system wasn't as defined; I was scared of the other man's voice but had pride enough always to have my own opinion. I could usually tell in the first couple of rounds how loud the other man was going to be and how silent I could make him.

There was one night in Ashburton, South Devon, which illustrates perfectly the terror of boxing and that most basic lesson of fighting: to turn your weaknesses to your advantage. I had travelled to the fight with my boyhood club, the Apollo, where several of our boys were to meet the Ashburton club's in the ring. I can't remember the real name of my opponent, but I do remember our trainer, Bert Sanders, telling me that he was known as the Fighting Farmer. Now, I may have scorned those from the countryside occasionally in jest, but I knew how all that manual labour could stack a boy like hay. I was concerned. Bert told me that it would be fine, that the ABA officials would make sure we were matched fairly and of the same weight class.

There were ten of us in the van to Ashburton with Bert driving. I was scheduled for the last bout of the night, so I thought I would get a chance to see the Fighting Farmer beforehand and reassure myself. Yet by the time my name was called I'd seen nothing of him. Bert offered ridicule, saying that he was most likely still milking the cows and I honestly thought he probably was. I climbed through the ropes, into my corner awaiting my first sight of this agricultural bruiser and immediately my sense of dread was confirmed. He was at least four inches taller and two stone heavier than I was. I thought that night perhaps the ABA were a malignant force conspiring against me, but Bert once again told me to sit tight and trust in the officials to make sure it was ok.

My mind clamoured for ways out, although inside I knew there was nothing that could be done without forfeiting my pride. And then came the announcement: 'Now for our final fight of the evening between Paul King of Torquay and the Fighting Farmer!' At least that's how I remember it. I'm sure they didn't say 'the Fighting Farmer', I'm sure they just said his name, but in my memory he always and forever will be, the Fighting Farmer. So when I recall that night, I remember the creaking Tannoy sounding as though it were reading a verse from the Book of Revelation, and one of the apocalyptic characters is always the Fighting Farmer. There was nothing for it: I had to fight.

Bert tried to soothe my fear and gave me that great southwest boxer, Bob Fitzsimmons' boxing proverb, 'The bigger the man, the heavier the fall.' Ruby Robert should have known, he boxed Jack Johnson and beat Gentleman Jim Corbett in his time. He was once the heavyweight champion of the world and the first boxer to be champion in three weight divisions. If anyone should have known, he should. But whatever Bert and Bob Fitzsimmons' wisdom, all I knew was a high concentration of terror was surging through me that night, but to match it I summoned an equal reserve of pride.

As the gong sounded, Bert shoved me forwards. What followed was the shortest fight I ever had and I can describe it the least well. For my memory of the moment was obliterated as soon as it was created and all I knew was that the Fighting Farmer lay prostrate on the canvas like a new born calf in the hay. I was shocked at the prescience of the old proverb, but supposed that the Freckled Wonder had seen plenty of nights like this. There was a count; I remember that. But the Apollo boys were already convinced; they didn't need to listen. Everyone was impressed. Even my father, who had turned up with a bunch of his mates in his taxi and denounced my chances, was the first and the biggest braggart, taking as much acclaim as he could for fathering such a punch. I was simply surprised, though I tried not to show it. I was even presented with a cup for the best performance of the night, quite a large one for the austere late 1940s.

My mother, though she had unwittingly inspired my first forays, never approved of my boxing. To someone who doesn't understand the sport it can sometimes seem foolish and wrongheaded, simply because it conjures up violence where there need not be any. They disregard the fact that it is highly controlled and most probably an escape channel for violence that will exist regardless. My mother had something of this opposition in her, intensified by a maternal desire to protect. Only once did I manage to coax her to come to a fight of mine and as a result it stands out in my memory as paradoxically, one to forget.

It was a sub-zero winter evening in Newton Abbot. I was fighting at the Butter Market and my mother had a ringside seat. I remember the boy I was to box was called Stevens and that he was a local and so had that extra home support. We were weighed in and then had to wait our turn, shivering, not on that occasion from fear but from cold, as we wore only vests, shorts and plimsolls. When it got closer to your fight, the officials would pull on your gloves and fasten them, checking that they were correct and hadn't been tampered with. It was at this point that my nerves would always begin and I would often feel the familiar pressure of my bladder on the lower part of my stomach. Sometimes, if I'd remembered to go earlier, I knew it was just nerves and could forget about it, pushing the sensation away with thought of the fight, but other times I knew that I couldn't hold on and if I didn't go it would be a big handicap. That night in Newton Abbot was one of them.

I quickly darted back towards the changing rooms where the toilets were located; the dirty white tiled corridors hung with condensation that was already turning to ice. I clumsily managed to drag the front of my shorts down, still wearing my boxing gloves. Direction was my biggest concern and my gloved thumbs the only appendage available. I grappled with my icicle, trying to hold back the unbearable urge that rises and is uncontrollable as soon as you have the knowledge that the toilet is close. In boxing gloves it was impossible; there was no need to flush afterwards.

After this struggle the bout didn't seem so daunting, but nevertheless the resulting fight went no way towards endearing boxing to my mother. It was the usual junior's amateur contest, with punches thrown like broken pistons come loose from their bracketing. There were only three rounds and then Stevens got a points decision; his home support screaming with delight. I don't know whether this reaction riled my mother and she felt humiliated at my loss, or that she was genuinely aggrieved at the fighting style, but as he climbed out of the ring, she screeched something at him and then clouted him round the head with her umbrella. I think I caught the words big and bully used in eloquent tandem. Angry words ensued as my delegation and the officials tried to calm Stevens' indignant supporters and spirit my mother out of the Butter Market. I almost announced my retirement from shame before I'd hardly begun.

My mother never came to a fight again. A few years later I saw Stevens in a dance hall and he accosted me, peering over my shoulder and saying, "Bloody hell, it's you! You haven't brought your mother, have yer? By Christ, I'd rather box you any day than her!" I told him I knew exactly what he meant.

Newton Abbot Butter Market

TORQUAY BOXER
TRIPLE CHAMP AT 17

Paul King, 17-years-old A.B.A. junior 10-stone, champion of Devon
Dorset and Cornwall, with Apollo Club trainer, Bert Sanders. King,
who is a keen member of the Apollo Club and the Torquay
Y.M.C.A., intends to enter for the senior championship this year.

CHAPTER 3

THE APOLLO

Before boxing became a drunken celebration, a salacious wellspring, or an aching disappointment, I remember it almost as an esoteric knowledge; something supposed to be secret and unavailable. This began before I had knocked out the Fighting Farmer or my mother had seen her one and only fight. It began as soon as I had been pessimistically told that boxing was an excellent lesson in the toughness of life, that it was practical and of use, not in itself, but because if you could use your fists then you had some worth. When I was young, more than anything I wanted to disbelieve this and I hoped that it was untrue. I was entranced and thought it the most desirable thing on earth to be involved in boxing.

I found myself, cocksure from the tuition I had received at school, becoming the street pedagogue on all matters boxing. Showing my friends how to stand in order to balance themselves and hold their body correctly, so that their arms would be effective as something other than limp flails; forcing their little brothers to participate in bouts as welter and flyweights whilst we fought as the heavyweights. Then we would award them the championship belt and they would be happy to get back to fighting by just slinging mud at each other.

One day, as a friend and I held one of our kerbside boxing tournaments, a mysterious man stopped his car to watch us play. After a short while, with a smile of patronage, he said that if we wanted to learn how to box properly then we should come to the hall on Dartmouth Road on Tuesday night and he would show us how. The man with the arcane knowledge was known as Snip

Cornish and I wondered what sort of exclusive club he ran. As well as being a pugilistic philosopher he was also a delivery driver for the local newspaper and his real name was Dennis. But when it came to boxing, that was irrelevant. I turned up the next Tuesday at the hall on Dartmouth Road and found myself outside a YMCA. I was sure that this couldn't be the right place and thought that maybe the mysterious man was playing with us and had sent us off for the fun of seeing how gullible we were.

To my surprise, inside I was greeted by a circus of sport, a few boys keeping a football up in one corner, some lifting weights in another and there in the centre, with bags and mats was Snip Cornish's dojo, as religiously placed as any martial arts school. He saw me, he recognized me and greeted me with the all the characteristic enthusiasm he seemed never without. Snip was serious and careful and knew what he was doing, but those days at the YMCA were unparalleled fun. He was well connected in the Torquay boxing sphere and when my strength became too much and I could outbox him, he graciously handed me up the ladder. That was when I was introduced to Bert Sanders and a club called the Apollo.

Sanders had been a professional himself in the 1920s and had gathered round him some excellent young boxers at the Apollo, which was located in Hele village. The Apollo certainly wasn't an architectural wonder, merely a green hut, but once inside things swung: punches and dances, all kinds of things were held there. Being able to do some boxing at school and then spending most evenings at either the YMCA or the Apollo, my life began to function on a diet of boxing. The Apollo was my first undiluted boxing world, dedicated to it alone. School was mere play and the YMCA had only half the knowledge and none of the intensity. At first the Apollo could put you into a terror, which was good training. You were exposed to absolute brutality and scenes that simply don't happen in most places and to most people. For one there were three fully graduated professionals there: George Pook,

TORQUAY APOLLO SPORTS CLUB'S BOXING TEAM

Centre Row (left to right) : T. Towler, J. Sterry, L. Harvey, M. Gregg, (next is face only of T. Crook), C. Bellingham, (at back in white is D. Stocker), B. Thomposn, (behind him is R. Marnely), C. Davies, T. Rourke, K. Jackson. Front Row : S. Banks (Asst. Trainer), P. King, Bert Sanders (Trainer). J. Mudge, J. Southwood (Team Secretary).

who was south west of England featherweight champion, and John O'Hagan and Dennis Cahill. If I thought the punch that flattened the Fighting Farmer was big, I only had to watch them spar to be reminded where it really lay on the scale. Watching them was like being let behind the veil, it was myth-busting; it placed reality where formerly only my imagination had been.

When I heard the trainers, with their strict Spartan ethic, forbidding their older charges from contact with females, I thought it some strange segregation specific to boxing. Then, when the trainers were not around, I would hear the unadulterated talk of the older boxers, who seemed unaware of my presence or that of any of the young boys. Not that they cared to be polite in order to protect our innocence, but when I listened I understood a clear contradiction and knew what it all meant. The trainers were the authority, but the older boxers were something to aspire towards and to imitate.

I also joined the army cadets, which was another place that boxing was actively encouraged. And it was in one of their competitions that I won my first boxing title, the nine-stone South-Western Counties, whilst representing Devon. As a youth, I was something of a sporting polymath; I ran for Torquay Athletic Club and, when the seasons were in, played cricket for the YMCA and football for my school. Though I was scared of the dogs I even used to go to the greyhound track with Uncle Sid, who trained them. But boxing was ever my love and I progressed at the Apollo enough to pick up the West of England junior ABA title, which covered Devon, Dorset and Cornwall.

I wasn't the only one at the Apollo who had begun to dance and swing with elegance. Under Bert we were the best boxing club in the West Country. For the town-hall tournaments we could draw a crowd of one thousand eight hundred and they'd have to put 'house full' signs up outside. We had home and away fixtures against top London clubs like Bourneville, Tate and Lyle and Silverton. We took on the Western Navy, and we beat them too. And the names! When something is that good then the names will never leave you: Johnny Mudge, Don Stocker, Reg Marnley, Alan Griffiths, Cyril Davies, Martin Gregg, Len Harvey, Basil Stoker, Ron Simms, John Sterry and, as moonlighters, Derek Darkie, Peter Mudge and Kurt Ernst.

Kurt Ernst. The only amateur to out-box me. He was all style and had the intelligence to use it; he gave me a beating four times. I would get too impatient with his games and he'd see a hole and bang, bang: a combination. He was behind my ears, like the part I always forgot to wash. Years later, as professionals, we found ourselves on the same bill in Leicester. I topped it; fought Rees Moore and won, and Kurt fought on the undercard against Darkie Hughes and was pummelled. Not because he was out-thought, it was simply blast after punishing blast, in which there is no knowledge, nothing secret or sacred, absolutely nothing mysterious. But this is what I came to discover, and it was very different from the imaginings I had when I first thought of boxing.

TORQUAY CLUB'S SUCCESS

Exeter and Exmouth Boxers Defeated

Squally winds and threatening clouds kept a number of people away from the open-air show held in connection with Torquay Carnival at the Recreation Ground on June 6. Those who risked the weather were treated to an interesting programme in which the local Apollo Club won their match against a team from Exmouth A. B. C. and Exeter A.C.F., by seven events to two. At the conclusion the Carnival Organiser, Mr. W. G. Speare, presented a silver cup to Paul King, captain of the winning team. King was a worthy winner of his bout with C. May (Exmouth) whose skilful boxing proved of little avail against the Torquay lad's terrific onslaughts.

CHAPTER 4

A GOOD SHOW

It was simple, unless you were partial to fighting men who didn't discriminate between fist and glass, there were two places you could fight: the town hall or the boxing booth. Of course, you fought in the gym too, but that was just practice; sparring and using bags. The real thing happened in only two places, the difference between which was not that of Butlins to Pontins, but of the English Riviera to the French. For a start there was the difference in respectability; the town hall had integrity, the sharp slash of the rules, the weight divisions, the competition. The idea that if you wanted to go somewhere as a boxer, if you had ambition, then you had to fight in the halls. But the boxing booths had that unauthorised excitement, not a little of which was due to the British Boxing Board of Control's prohibition of its registered fighters from boxing in them. That was in 1947. I was sixteen, had never heard of the boxing booths and, like some kind of fateful crossing of opposing trajectories, that very same year, I was introduced to their amateur thrill. As the amateurs were forced from the booths, so the garish lights shone at fewer and fewer fairgrounds. I was there at the beginning of the end, as the booths slowly regressed into memory.

My own introduction to the booths took place one evening during the summer. I had heard that the fair was in town, but I wasn't interested. I happened to be promenading along the waterfront in Torquay with my girlfriend Pam, when we chanced upon my trainer from the Apollo, Bert. It was almost as if he had been looking for me. "Fancy earning some money, young 'un? There's a fair in town looking for boxers for the booths." I hesitated and Bert tried to reassure me by telling me it would be a gee. It didn't work,

Fairground, Torquay, 1954

I didn't know what a gee was. So he gave me the insider's knowledge, telling me that booth boxers, the men you challenged to a fight, were not there to lay you out flat at the first opportunity, they were showmen and businessmen, not just pure fighters. He said they would go easy on you if you wanted, and box with shackled wrists, because the crowd were not there to see a man get punched out in the first round, they wanted to believe the men who got up to fight could stand up for themselves. The simple principle was: the crowd wanted to see a good fight and were willing to pay for it, so it was in the interests of those who ran the booth to put on a show. If they did this believably then the nobbins would flow freely. I didn't know what nobbins were and I hesitated to ask. However, Pam did it for me. "Nobbins is the money the crowd toss into the ring." Pam was dubious, but her feminine concern was mere tinder to my contrariness.

So, as the hawkers say, we rolled up, the three of us, and were regaled with that noise, that purely English noise of the fairground: the high harpsichord waltz and the round organ, the barkers and their patter. We whirled through colours and lights, Bert leading like a train, unvarying in his route, Pam hanging from my arm as though if she let go she would fall into an abyss. Before any chance of properly acquainting myself with the fairground, before even a mutual doff of the cap, I found myself at the front of the crowd in the boxing booth and staring into faces the like of which I had never before seen. Boxing faces. Who ran the boxing booth? Had they, in the dead of night, committed profane acts and ripped the gargoyles from the walls of Exeter Cathedral, corralling and coercing them to fight on the fairground circuit? The reds and the greens of the lights were smeared across these boxing faces, but recesses and wrinkles, gothic noses and ecclesiastical ears darkened their aspects. The creeping fear that had begun its slow slink through my mind as we first approached the fairground had accelerated and was now rampaging.

The spieler, the ringmaster, was bawling: he preached at the crowd, heckled their frailties, tilted with their egos, turned the heat on their testosterone until it boiled. "Where is the local boy who will challenge our champ Emlyn Jones undefeated in fourteen fights? Where is the man brave enough? Who is the key to Torquay?" Bert was behind me, his finger pointing down at the top of my head. The spieler's eyes, wild and libertine, met the finger's vertical line and his scarlet face fixed upon my white face. He smiled a beckoning fairground smile and wheeled away to his microphone "Here he is, Ladies and Gentlemen! Our local boy." I was petrified out of any reaction.

Sam McKeown's Boxing Booth

Before I go on, let me tell you a little story about this spieler, the man who had announced me as 'Our Local Boy'. I would soon know this man and I would know him as Mr Jack Turner. He was an ex-fighter and thankfully had been mediocre with the gloves on. For a man with his lack of compassion would have been a terrible affliction on the human race if he had been endowed with any real power. There was a pal of mine, Frank, who I had met on the booths and whom I liked very much. On one occasion, without his usual fitness and with an unusual pudge, Frank had travelled up to fight on the booth at Barnstaple. Unfortunately, he was challenged by a Navy man and was torn down early in the fight by an anchor of a right, plumb on the chin. He must have been out before gravity even had the chance to do its work.

We hurriedly carried him out of the ring and out of sight; it was a sin to let the punters see lingering pain, the kind that might cause revulsion and an immediate distaste for violence. Jack Turner thought it was bad for business. "An injured boxer is not a boxer, he's an invalid. People don't come to the booths to see freaks, they come to see fights. The oddballs and uglys are at the other side of the fairground. Take 'em there, or take 'em home!" But all of us knew that Frank was concussed. However, Jack Turner only ever had one remedy for an injury: a bucket of cold water over the head. And this was Frank's treatment.

After his soaking, Frank managed to flicker his eyelids a little but was clearly having trouble with coherent thought and spatial judgement. Jack Turner didn't flinch. He fiddled in his pocket, took out some coins, pressed them into my hand and spat "Here, take this and him on the Bournemouth train." I couldn't understand Jack's callousness. "What? I can't just put him on the train! You can see he's barely conscious." Jack didn't care. "Hark at the little angel. If you don't like seeing heads getting knocked, what are you doing boxing?"

At least he gave Frank his train fare. I dressed him and we took a taxi to the station. I helped him into a carriage and asked a middle-aged man sitting opposite where he was bound, with the intention of enlisting his assistance. Finding that he was to change at Bristol, I told him Frank had fallen and hit his head and that he had to get home to Bournemouth tonight as he had to wake early to do his milk-round tomorrow morning. Would the gentleman please ensure that Frank changed at Bristol for the Bournemouth train and perhaps pass him to a helpful guard? The man looked at Frank and hesitated. I took my opportunity, quickly stepped backwards off the train and thanked him. He got up to say something, but I was already walking away and have no idea what it was. That was the last time I ever saw Frank. One of Jack Turner's favourite aphorisms seems to sum it up, he would always say, as if delighting in his self-service "It's a tough life, especially if you're employed by Jack Turner."

And right now, it seemed I was. Jack Turner had announced me. People looked on with smirks that seemed pregnant with a knowledge I had not yet encountered, but which I soon would. Bert propelled me forwards to the bottom of some steps, which led up to a platform on which those gargoyles stood. Jack Turner bent down and asked my name. "Paul King." I replied. He swung himself back to his microphone and stuttered his rhetoric incredulously at the crowd, "What? What's this? He thinks he can knock our fighter out!" The crowd whistled and laughed and seemed to inflate thunderously. I mounted the steps in pursuit and tried to rebuke him: "What are you doing? I didn't say that!" But Jack was coming loose now. He held the microphone away from me and unravelled his spiel, "Ladies and Gentlemen, we have a cocky lad with us today! Not only does he predict a knock-out; he's so confident that he wants to put money on it!" And I thought I'd come to the fair to make money.

I felt exposed. I looked around in hope for the abyss Pam had been trying to avoid earlier, but all I saw was a slab of granite. I wondered what sort of black magic could have animated it, squeezed it into shorts and taught it to box. I looked out towards the crowd and caught Pam's eye. I knew that our thoughts ran parallel; I think that was our closest moment in the whole time we were together.

As Jack Turner continued delivering his driving spiel to the crowd and more of those outside were drawn in, I was taken out the back and gloves were strapped to me. I am not ashamed to say that I approached Emlyn Jones as apologetically and meekly as if it was my first day at school; I tried to make amends for Jack Turner's misrepresentation. "Excuse me, but I didn't say those things about knocking you out and wanting to bet money on it."Jones was gentler than I had expected, "Don't worry, son, it's Jack working up the crowd, we're trying to make money here." That was the businessman Bert had told me about; I would soon see Jones' showman too.

Standing in the ring opposite this man, whose formidable flanks seemed thicker than my torso, I hoped that I could trust his reassurance. The gong went and we began by trading a few blows. It was just like a sparring session and I began to relax slightly. In the second round things began to move a little and became more hectic. As we were in a clinch Jones told me to take a count; he had begun to engineer the fight and I deferred, not wishing upset him. The gong went and I returned to my corner. As the reality of the booths became clear to me, I remember a rush of confidence, it seemed easy and the nerves I had before seemed now as illusory as I knew the fight was going to be. Three more minutes, I thought, and I'm off with a couple of quid in my pocket.

At the beginning of the third round Jones told me to hit him on the jaw. First I gave him a few punches to block and then started opening up. But when it came to it, the punch, the one he'd asked for, was more likely to hurt my fist than his face. He went down and I felt the canvas momentarily tauten beneath my feet. The count began and his great, stony bulk whimpered and shuddered like a great old engine struggling to start; he just managed to rise at nine. After the emotions that had tumbled through me before the fight I couldn't help but feel that it was all quite pathetic, that this man now quivered in frailty after such a meagre expansion of energy. But this was his showmanship. Only he and I knew the fierceness of the punch. The crowd had no idea and they went berserk as the gong resounded and the fight was ended. Jack Turner came over to me: "Well done, lad. Just stay put for a second." He strode to the centre of the ring and ran himself through his mike again, "Ladies and gentlemen, Paul King has just told me that over the longer distance of four rounds he will knock Jones out for sure!" And before I knew it, after I had thought it was all over, I was in for another fight.

Jack Turner certainly knew what he was doing with a microphone in his hand. He raked his throat and shouted at the crowd outside, telling people what excitement and drama they'd missed; how I'd knocked the professional down in the third round and now there was a grudge that had to be resolved. People bottlenecked at the booth entrance and inside the crowd were swelling like a black eye. I don't know whether it was the burgeoning crowd or whether it was my own sense of confusion at having to rapidly face another bell, but my second fight had a different, more hostile, atmosphere. There were no words to sooth or instruct this time and, by God, I had to fight. It was all I could do to hold Jones off, just to stay on my feet. I went down twice and had him on the floor for a short count but by the end of it all, when the final gong went and the grudge was announced to have been settled, my veins ran with pure relief.

Jack Turner was delighted and he flirted with me for the money I could bring him; he asked if I was interested in turning professional. I muttered something about the nicety professionals enjoy of getting paid and he smiled at the kindred thought. He amplified his voice once more and told the crowd, "This young lad has put up such a courageous fight I am going to allow him the

privilege of passing amongst you with the hat. Give all you can for the fight he put up". A sailor lent his cap and Emlyn Jones stood behind me shouting at the crowd, telling them what an opponent I'd been and coaxing them to be free with their generosity. He kept calling me the local lad. I was pushed round the ring and made to offer the hat to all. They willingly responded and soon I had to hold the hat with two hands as it wilted under the weight of the coins.

I greedily retreated to the back of the booth and lent over the money like a miser, tallying it up in my head as coin fell upon coin. The people of Torquay were good to their own and I smiled at the ten pounds fragmented and heaped in front of me. In my innocence and excitement I was about to thrust the whole lot into my pockets, when Jones reminded me, in a faintly menacing way, that it had been a cast production and not a one man show. "I went easy on you," he said as he formulated a fifty-fifty split.

As I sauntered out of the booth and into the fairground I could feel how Jones had tenderised my eye and made my lip fat. As I strolled around I felt benevolence towards the world that the abatement of the violent surge had given me. The menagerie, the wall of death, the freak shows, illusion booths, puppetry, the rides and game stalls. If the fairground ever had any moral stricture it was its distaste for orthodoxy. It was a triumph for the kind of weirdness that normal people brand as dangerous; some went for fun, some went to gawp, I went for nourishment.

During the fighting and hollering Pam had walked out of my mind and I couldn't find her anywhere in the booth. I finally came across her hurling balls ferociously at coconuts. "Oh," she said "I thought I heard an ambulance about half an hour ago. I assumed it was for you." She had lost interest in me. She said she hadn't even seen the first fight. But it didn't matter for I had found a new love that night. We walked back to town together and made no declaration of it, but slipped away in mutual silence.

My father had no such unspoken eloquence and when I got home he gave me an open palm across the head. Didn't I know that I could get thrown out of amateur boxing for fighting in a booth? He called me an idiot and a thick head and wondered if there was any brain inside and if it wasn't just all bone from neck to scalp. "If anyone asks, I'll tell them it was you then." I said as I motioned towards my black eye. But none of what he said or what Pam thought moved me, I was overcome. It was a revelation that no amount of reasoning or logic or persuasion could displace. The fairground had my emotion and that was enough.

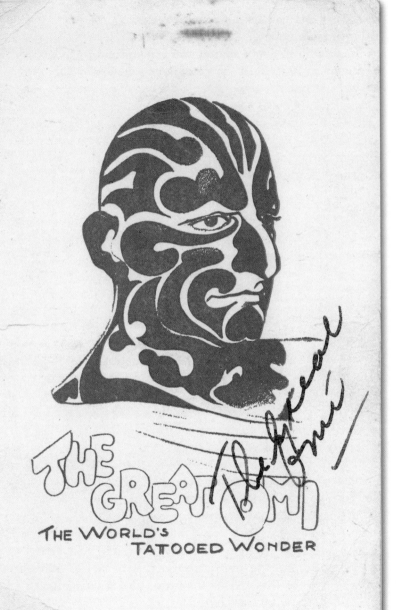

THE GREAT OMI

THE WORLD'S TATOOED WONDER

CHAPTER 5

LIFE ON THE BOOTHS

There is hardly a town in the West Country I haven't fought in. St Austell, Totnes, Teignmouth, Dawlish, Weston-super-Mare, Bude, St Ives; I performed on the booths until I was halfway across Hampshire. The individuals who were attracted to life in this travelling village held the most fascination for me. They were as far from average as you care to go, attracted by the living they could make from their strangeness or moulded by the exposure of being born amongst it all. Nowhere else would you meet them in such abundance.

One of the most impressive of characters was the Great Omi. A war hero, he spun his trade as 'the most tattooed man on earth around its full circumference'. I can imagine the strange mix of wonder and condescension of those who paid to see his aberrant form, a parent saying to a child, look son, how can a person do that to their body? It's the only one God gave them. And then I imagined the Great Omi dwelling on the experience that engendered his need be covered in tattoos; of the Great War where he had fought in Mesopotamia and of the bodies he must have seen in a state far more grotesque than anyone could now consider his. Nations usually honour their war heroes, and yet these people came to gawp at Omi and to disapprove once their titillation was satiated. However, I knew his tattoos had a story and I could imagine him a young man in the war, faceless because he was amongst so many other young men who shared his endeavors. For me, the best tattoo was the one he had on his back: a full hunt scene that chased the fox until it disappeared into its hole. All that was tattooed of the fox was his brush.

For some the fairground was a necessary lifestyle rather than a choice. One of these was Maria, a trapeze artist, who I fell in love with. She was of Italian ancestry and was truly beautiful. After taking her out one evening she invited me back to her family's caravan, a huge honour for a flattie. For that's what I was labelled; the fairground had its own divisions and flatties were non-permanents, outsiders who had been allowed in to the fold. The majority of others were members of the Showmen's Guild, which offered a certain status. The Guild was founded over a hundred years ago to protect and further the interests of travelling showmen both on and off the fairground. Their members were proud people, they had to be, due to all the prejudice they suffered. So it was a serious decision to invite an outsider into the family caravan; the inner sanctum.

I met Maria's mother, who had also been a trapeze artist, but now was frail and bedridden. Maria told me that some years ago her grip had failed her and she had fallen, breaking her back. After suffering such a horrific accident I naively wondered how Maria's mother could let Maria continue with the same act. Thinking about it, perhaps it was because there were little or no other prospects for Maria. Growing up on a fairground she only had a spattering of conventional education and would have faced prejudice in the outside world. Maybe it was as son follows father down the pit or into the factory or mill, just the familiar cycle of necessity, of having no other option. And there was never more of a family business than those that ran the fairgrounds. I remember Maria's mother asking, during my visit if I was Catholic and when I said no, she said "Ah, what a shame. Such a nice boy too."

As Maria's family had grown into the itinerant lifestyle of the fairs there were also those whose ancestors had always been wayfarers. These were the gypsies, they lived on the fair and owned a great many of the stalls, and they produced such incongruities as calling the biggest and strongest of their masculine number Katie.

The irony was certainly not lost on him. But, unsurprisingly, it failed to touch a group of Scottish soldiers who visited the fair one day in Alton, Hampshire. From what I heard they had found Katie's bean stall, asked for the owner and, without setting eyes upon him, had learnt that his name was Katie and seen the chance for their wit to shine. The word was passed around that they had threatened to return mob-handed, which was when I heard of the altercation. The gypsies, unruffled and showing not a sign of being intimidated started to prepare. If the Scots were going to return in numbers, they would need at least two full divisions.

The soldiers did indeed pay a second visit to the fairground the next day. They arrived with swelled ranks, loud and confrontational. I was standing outside the booth when they surged in amongst the rows of stalls and began jostling people, punters too, and snatching things from the food stalls. Suddenly, as if silently secreted from behind the stalls, gypsies, armed with staves and iron bars and at least one old rifle, appeared. They set up an implacable defence, roused a caustic racket and advanced upon the Scots, who ran away in all directions. No blood was spilled. There was just a simple refusal to be cowed by intimidation and it exposed the soldiers' bluff. The fairground community and the gypsies, perhaps because they were so used to having no other barrier between themselves and open hostility, certainly knew how to protect themselves.

This is more than can be said for most of the average blokes who volunteered to fight on the booths, where public participation was a necessity. There were always grandiose loudmouths in the audience, heckling and belittling the challenge of taking up a pair of gloves. And yet it was a real rarity that they would actually follow their voices and fight, because they knew that they would be getting in the ring with someone who is trained to box. Their blustering was simply a manifestation of huge ego; an ego that didn't want to be humiliated. But what they failed to understand

was that to lose was only a humiliation if expectations were not met. Not that boxers want to lose, they will try their absolute utmost not to, but if they do then they will be consoled by the knowledge that to merely get in the ring was an achievement in itself.

Of course, if a boxer of repute, fighting a man who can only punch effectively with one hand, gets knocked down and beaten, he should rightly feel humiliated, but this is an extreme example. However, the situation was the same for these raconteurs; they would brag so much that people would have expectations of them, their friends; the crowd; even the other boxers. This meant that when the reality of the fight was upon them, failure would disappoint and being a disappointment can be humiliating. Consequently, the booth boys would never go easy on a loud-mouth. There is however, always an exception to the rule, and generally the exceptions are much more interesting than the herd. I came across one such exception on a fair at Southampton Common. The man was typical in the sense that he simply wouldn't shut-up, but he was so persistent and annoying that Jack Turner invited him to climb into the ring before he had even got to the part of his speech where he asks for volunteers.

The first unusual thing this man did was accept. Although I had every intention of showing him the colour of his own blood, I gave him the usual surrendering speech; asking if he wanted me to go easy on him. The second unusual thing he did was reject my offer. He mustered some menace and beady eyed, said "I'm going to kill you." My first reaction was surprise. Most challengers were supplicating and glad to discover that they wouldn't be pummelled without mercy. This man seemed to be operating because of some sort of grudge. His arrogance was wretched, it caused me to feel

Opposite picture (left to right): Jimmy Jury, Battling Jojo, Albert Cann, Bob Turner, Reg Ballinger, Joe Underwood, Pat McKeown, Freddie Mills.

repugnance and to want to hurt him even more. I planned to flatten him as quickly as possible and to humiliate him in the most withering way. The third unusual thing this man did was move. It turned out that the loudmouth could box. He was quick, well balanced and knew how to form an effective guard. Knowing to extend his arm so that the full force of his muscles was centred upon his knuckles was the fourth thing that was far from usual about him. In the first two rounds I could barely touch him. In the break between the second and third, Jack Turner was threatening to give him my wages and job. But to show what a genial employer he was, Turner offered me advice on how to forestall this loss. He told me to punch straight, first a right, then a left. I was firmly a hook man, it was easily my best punch and I was doubtful that throwing an unspecialised punch would have much effect if my best was being so easily rebuffed.

However, Jack must have seen something I hadn't, because when I tried his advice, a tight right clipped him and then a bird-like left flew straight through and knocked him out. Jack counted ten and he did not flicker an eyelid. He was quickly taken out of sight and the familiar bucket of icy water poured over his head. He had fought as if he had learnt the rudiments. If only someone had trained him more, he surely could have gone professional. That I have always been convinced of; his ability was as natural as the gem-patterns formed in rocks; he could have been a champion.

Not that the booths hadn't been tramped by their fair share of champions. There was Tiger Shark, who would parade a belt in front of the crowd. The spieler told them that it was the belt of the heavyweight champion of the Far East and the only way to question its validity was to box Tiger Shark and see him prove it with his fists. Or Roy 'Bull' Davies, the consummate gentleman of the ring, who was from Plymouth and claimed to have been the boxing champion of his POW camp in the war, fighting both Russian prisoners and German guards. Or Trevor Burt, who wasn't a champion himself but had fought with the best of them.

He was a cruiserweight and had been in the ring with Freddie Mills; the way he told it, on his wedding day. Or Taff, who was always known by his patriotic nickname so that his real name became subsumed, like waste on a rubbish heap.

Taff had been on the booth that day in 1947 when I had fought Emlyn Jones. He was always promoted as being the middleweight champion of Wales, which, unlike the champ of the Far East, held more likeness to reality, and we never questioned it. His billing continued throughout the years until it seemed unlikely that he still was, if he had ever been. When I first met him, I had no doubt that he was the middleweight champion of Wales, he became for me, with his abstract nose and equilateral shoulders, the purified essence of boxing. He never trained, but had an organically manufactured physique, enough to intimidate you from the opposite corner of the ring. And, at intervals, when an educational urge overcame him, he would teach me insidious little moves, like how to slip and duck and hold your opponent to give yourself time for a rest.

When my life took me away from the booths, I lost touch with him for a time, until I paid a visit to the fair at Poole. I had become a professional and was in the surge of new energy, under the optimism of possibility. I didn't recognise any of the people I saw on the booth at first and was content to stand and watch. The spieler said something about a Welsh middleweight champion, who had once been at the top of his profession, and was waiting in the back for anyone who was brave enough to challenge him. Immediately I thought of Taff and, pushing to the front, I spoke to one of the booth boys. I inquired about Taff, being careful not to mention 'the Welsh middleweight champion' for fear that the boy would take it as a challenge and inform the spieler, whereupon I would have to meet an old friend with gloves on or extricate myself from an embarrassing situation. The boy led me behind the booth and I saw the dusty frame of an old man, who turned and looked at me with dull eyes until he recognised me and I recognised him. It was Taff.

He had lost his old suppleness of shape. In the absence of training, time had begun to warp his legs, so that he now scratched a rhythm on the ground with his toes as he walked. We went for a stroll around the fairground to tell new tales and ruminate on old ones. But the main narrative that Taff told was a tragedy. His managers had promised him the earth and naively he had believed them. However, nothing that they said had come to pass and he'd lost his wife because of it. Some of it had happened before I'd met him; most of it however, I hadn't heard. Now all he had of his own was a bunk at the back of the booth, and even that was loaned. He told his biography as a fable, of what he saw as the sport's degradation of its once quintessential performers. The moral was a warning: to get out of boxing early enough. I remember feeling it to be melodrama, an exaggeration. But then I was young and had no time for pessimism.

During this time I was living in Bournemouth and kept in touch with Taff. After the fair had finished, he managed to get a job as a porter in a Poole hotel. In the autumn I paid him a visit and after his shift we went to a small café for cake and tea. To my relief, his composition had begun to run with more colour again. He told me how he was enjoying working at the hotel. His natural affability, the instant fraternity he inspired and the ability to always strike hidden humour, had made him popular with customers and his bosses. The following year I attempted to contact Taff again, in the only way I knew how (he never had a telephone), by going to the hotel. I was informed that he had left a few months previously, giving only a week's notice and no indication as to his motivation or destination. So, barring another coincidental meeting like the one at Poole fair, Taff was lost to me and I heard neither whisper nor shout of him again. All I had left was an inexplicable mystery, no clues, no go-betweens. In Taff's case I didn't even have his full name. The individual who disappears in the boundless expanse of humanity is the most daunting mystery there is.

PART TWO

TRADING PUNCHES FOR MONEY

Training, Army 9th Regiment

CHAPTER 6

TRADING PUNCHES FOR MONEY

I turned professional in the final days of my National Service. After two years of enforced servitude I was eager to reacquaint myself with civilian life. I had done well in the army, a few months in I had managed to use my athleticism to obtain a position as a Personal Training Instructor, and from then on I had experienced the more desirable side of military life.

I received a letter at camp from Jack Turner informing me of the arrangements for my first professional bout, which was to take place at Connaught Drill Hall in Portsmouth; my induction amongst the pugilist merchants who traded punches for money. I read that I would be appearing on the same bill as well known names, names that could attract a crowd.Youthful awe filled me and I was completely compliant. I would travel anywhere I was told, get there by any method I could and box anyone who faced me from the opposite corner. The timing was also fortuitous as my amateur boxing had just been curtailed for a second time, again by a ban for fighting on the booths.

Beforehand I was extremely nervous, not because I feared the other man, but because it was my beginning. From now there would be a record with my name on it that would forever detail how good a boxer I was and I was anxious not to soil it so soon. I was to box a Cockney called Johnny Burns. He had lost his first two fights and then seemed to find out how the gloves swung and he'd won and then won again. I imagined his changing room beforehand, his manager in his face, telling him that I was his hat-trick man; beat me and it would be a sign, something more than just psychological momentum.

Perhaps the desire for an unblemished record was stronger than the desire for a hat-trick of wins, or perhaps because I was simply a better boxer than Johnny Burns, but the fight only lasted four rounds. I received my five pounds winning fee, which quite honestly, with a good crowd, I could have earned on the booths. But this was real boxing, full of talented fighters, not just showmanship and money making. Here committed boxing fans came to watch, not just the curious who chanced by a booth on their way to a coconut shy; even great boxers would come to measure the newly cut muscle. In the crowd my first night was Joe Beckett, a former heavyweight champion of England and a Romany. I met him afterwards and he told me that he thought I had some future. Maybe he was just being polite, a benign master too generous not to encourage. Back then, in the happiness of victory, the thought that he could be insincere never passed through my mind.

Later, when all the well-wishers had vanished, I stepped out of the drill hall into the August night, now as chilled as a winter month, and with the cold came the realisation that I had made no plan to get back to camp at Farnham South Cove. The army, in their understanding, had let me out, but they also expected me back; I could not stay on the coast. By this time the last train had already gone and all I could do was hitchhike. With kit-bag slung over my shoulder I set out for a road that led north out of Portsmouth and raised my thumb as a flag of friendship to every passing vehicle. When, finally someone stopped, it was the most unlikely of beasts, a Rolls Royce gliding through the night like velvet. The philanthropic driver asked after my story, as all good hitchhikers should offer in lieu of payment, and thankfully I didn't have to use any imagination. I told him that he chauffeured a professional boxer on the night of his inaugural bout, which of course, had been won. I don't know if it was because of this, but generously he dropped me right outside the camp gates. I was disappointed that no one had been there to see it.

JIMMY MILLER
the Falmouth welterweight

PAUL KING'S FIRST PROFESSIONAL BOUT

Paul King, Torquay amateur welterweight makes his professional debut at Plymouth on August 13 when he meets Jimmy Miller at Falmouth in a six rounds supporting contest in the programme headed by the British Empire lightweight clash between Cliff Anderson (British Guiana) and Emmett Kenny (St. Helens). King is managed by Jack Turner, the man who originally "discovered" Freddie Mills.

Paul King, 20-years-old, at one time Torquay's leading amateur welterweight, makes his professional debut tonight when he meets J. Burns (London), at Portsmouth. King will meet Jimmy Miller of Falmouth, at Plymouth on August 13.

My second fight came quickly. Only five days later I was travelling down to Devon and Plymouth to box Jimmy Miller. After the felicity of my first fight, I remember this one as a much greater agony. I did not lose, I did not draw and neither was I injured. Yet my physical being felt like it had spent years being ravaged by disease. I thought that it must be what consumption feels like. I had won a points decision, but Jimmy had punished me for it. As people congratulated me I barely registered their words and I thought that if Joe Beckett had been there that night, no amount of politeness would have been able to coax him into lauding my prospects. Despite the beating we gave each other, I remained friends with Jimmy for years afterwards and eventually I told him the truth of how I'd felt after our fight. He said that if he did nothing else, he wanted that as the epitaph on his tombstone.

The early months of my professional boxing career were not the most organised, nor were they the most conducive to maintaining peak condition. I had no permanent training facilities, I wasn't sparring as much as I should or with the boxers I should and I didn't even have a proper boxing coach. There was no one to show me the habits of boxing, the nuances that aren't obvious, which only serious boxing men know and that don't exist for the average person. Most men equate boxing with fighting and fighting with strength and speed and toughness; the powerful punch, the quick reactions and the durable chin. Boxing however, is so much more than that. It is exact and meticulous. When you hear that Rocky Marciano never trained for less than two months before each fight you know that it has something of pure, monkish asceticism about it. As it was I could only learn through experience and anecdote. Whenever I met an old fist I would ply them with questions on how they operated until they looked ready to demonstrate on me for real. But it wasn't the same as a methodical and considered approach. This may seem contrary to those who believe in adrenaline and the heat of battle, but why else did Marciano train for months beforehand? Certainly not to leave it to instinct alone.

★ ★ ★ ★

A Freddie Lawson - George Harrison Presentation

★ ★ ★ ★

EIGHT ROUNDS MIDDLEWEIGHT

Sammy MILSOM v. Eddie WEBB
(RADSTOCK)   (JAMAICA)

EIGHT ROUNDS LIGHTWEIGHT

Cyril EVANS v. Peter INDACO
(WELWYN)   (BRIXTON)

SIX ROUNDS MIDDLEWEIGHT

Bob JOHNSON v. Pat GAMBLE
(PLYMOUTH)   (DEVONPORT)

SIX ROUNDS WELTERWEIGHT

Paul KING v. Jimmy MILLER
(TORQUAY)   PAUL   WON   (FALMOUTH)

EIGHT ROUNDS LIGHT-HEAVYWEIGHT

Gene FOWLER v. Sammy WILDE
(CANADA)   (NIGERIA)

(All Rounds of Three-Minutes Duration).

The Gloves used in all Lawson — Harrison Promotions

ARE SPECIALLY MADE BY

BAILY'S of GLASTONBURY

Sole Makers of the World-famous " GLASTONBURY GLOVE "

★ ★ ★ ★

The army taught me the benefit of determination and persistence, but alone they are attributes that can assist only a gravedigger or a furniture mover. I needed formulae and physics. In the beginning, my style was straight out of the Great War; I really didn't know what I was doing but I was throwing all I had into it anyway. As an amateur I had the skill to out-box fighters who didn't use ideas, but when it came to professionalism I found myself fighting like Terry Downes used to when we were kids. I'd swing hooks with nothing more than hope behind them and find, because I'd begun so fast, that I couldn't let up or I would be bereft of direction. There was no speed play to what I did, just an over-whelming swarm of buzzing punches. It certainly wasn't dull for spectators, but I felt the vulnerability of the stage, like an actor who goes from church halls to the West End and finds the extra heat of the lights makes him damper than he ever was before. It was also exacerbated by my age. I was younger than most of the boxers I fought and I always assumed experience had taught them more than it had time to teach me. Yet, despite the shortcomings in my training, by the time of my sixth fight against Joe Pring, I hadn't spilt a drop of ink on my card.

In between the Miller and Pring fights I got my first recognition in the press. The local newspaper called my fight against Owen Randall, again to be held in Plymouth, a 'stiff test'. The reporter must have been spying in on Randall's training to land such an exclusive. Nevertheless, my father cut it out and proudly posted it on his kitchen wall. There were two former champions going at each other that night too, Bos Murphy and Henry Hall, who were still trying to knock another man's teeth out and take a wage for doing it. Murphy was a Kiwi, he'd been the Empire middleweight champion for a couple of fights before losing it to Dick Turpin. He would win in Plymouth, but it would be his last. He retired after losing his next fight. Hall was a Steel City man and had been the British welter champion for most of 1949 before moving up a division. He wouldn't win a fight again and retired the following year. Both boxers were nearing the end of their careers. They must have been able to feel it in their fibre, but they still slugged monstrously so that watching them, I could see far back to their beginning whilst witnessing their end.

Watching this fight gave me a heightened sense of self-importance that I took into the ring with me against Owen Randall. I focused my delight at the roughness of my new profession into an equally rough showing of boxing skill. My hooks, whipping as fast as a cat-o-nine tales, were there, but Randall had experience and kept closing in and crowding me out. He cut me in the third, but he couldn't open it enough for it to be a hindrance and I managed to keep my momentum turning enough to win on points. The four thousand people in the crowd and the Mayor of Plymouth clearly enjoyed it, but it was another dirty display and I knew that type of boxing could only take me so far. However, I had beaten Randall once, so why not do it again a month later? I managed to defeat him on points again, but this time at the Colston Hall, a beautiful Bristol Byzantine building that I would revisit several times, not least for two fights against Joe Pring.

Pring was a coalman from Bristol. He had only fought two professional bouts before we met, but he'd been boxing at the highest amateur level for enough time to make him a mature fighter compared to myself. Plus he'd started out professionally unbeaten. Perhaps he'd had enough of what the coal dust was doing to his lungs and taken his talent into the professional ring. It seemed that hard industrial labour had stretched him in every direction, so much so that I felt I'd need a coal-pick to defeat such a huge a man. I clearly remember the worry I had before the fight, exacerbated because we were fighting in his home city and he had the crowd on his side.

Colston Hall was a city hall, a full pint glass of an arena compared to the halves that I was used to. When it came to the sound of the bell I didn't charge forward bull-like as I normally did, I reared onto hind legs as a frightened horse might do and wheeled my

| MONDAY, 17th NOVEMBER | Colston Hall | At 7.30 p.m. Doors open: 6.30 p.m. |

Colston Hall

MONDAY, 17th NOVEMBER — At 7.30 p.m. Doors open: 6.30 p.m.

COLSTON HALL ENTERTAINMENTS COMMITTEE

Promoter: **Tom Pyper** Matchmaker: **Jack Turner**

PRESENT: # BOXING

Sensational 8 Three Min. Rounds Welterweight Contest at 10st. 10lbs.
under forfeit

Terry Ratcliffe

(Bristol)

Now in Championship form. Recently caused a sensation at the Harringay Arena by his knock-out of the undefeated Irish Welter Weight Bunty Adamson. Ratcliffe showed Championship class and can be matched with any British Welter Weight

VERSUS

Eric Billington

(Liverpool)

Regarded as great a prospect in the North as Ratcliffe in the West. K.O.'d Carl Johnson of Jamaica. Had great contests with Bunty Adamson of Belfast and Israel Boyle.

WEIGH-IN at 1.0 p.m. PUBLIC INVITED. Licensed by B.B.B. of C. (1929)

Special Six 3 Min. Rounds Middleweight Bout at 10st. 2lbs.

Bryn JONES
(Bristol)
Splendid local prospect

v.

Alf LAYE
(London)
A.B.A. Champion 1951

Grand All-action Return Challenge Welterweight Contest at 10st 8lbs.
Eight 3 Min. Rounds

PAUL KING
(Torquay)
The brilliant Torquay Ex-Amateur Undefeated since turning pro and regarded by experts as a great prospect

JOE PRING
(Bristol)
Pring is in special training for this return bout. Draw with King at the Colston Hall in a thrilling contest. He is confident he can defeat King - hence his challenge

---

Grand Six 3 Min. Rounds Lightweight Contest at 9st. 8lbs.

Laurie HENRY
(Jamaica)
All-action coloured fighter

v.

Len GRAINGER
(Bristol)
Rapidly improving local Lightweight

Six 2 Min. Rounds Heavyweight Contest

CLIFF PURNELL v. **SID DURSTON**
(Bath)   (Bridgwater)

These two young Heavyweights had a great slam at the last show

---

All-Action Middleweight Contest at 11st. 8lbs.

JOHNNY BYRNES v. **DUDLEY COX**
(Bristol)   (Bournemouth)

Has been showing splendid form and is out to get to the top this season. Remember his last bout at this venue when he stopped Johnny Mudge of Torquay in a thrilling contest

Tough, rugged young Middleweight. In his last contest here stopped Richard Corbett in a hectic bout. Has defeated amongst others —Bobby Fish, Eddy Clancey, Arthur Stone, Fred Ballio. Cox has never been knocked out

---

Tickets: 30/-, 21/-, 15/-, 10/6, 7/6 & 5/-
From COLSTON HALL BOOKING OFFICE (Phone 21768)
Also MILTON'S LIBRARY, CO-OP STORES, CASTLE STREET & C.W.S. TRAVEL BUREAU, BROAD QUAY

PRINTED BY THE CORPORATION

arms like uncontrolled hooves. It was a different style, but not the one I wanted. My inexperience had left me without any idea of what to do. We boxed the full six rounds that night and my disappointment in myself became inflated as I gradually realised that Pring was as poor a tactician as me. At the end of the fight the referee was so upset, as if we'd killed his sport, that he refused to raise either of our arms and called it a draw.

After the Pring fight, when people talked about me, they would speak of a shower that had failed to develop into a deluge. In a sport powered by testosterone the critics matter, an insult is untenable if a reputation is to stay untouched, but then everyone knows this. After five wins without failure there was an ugly capital D that ruptured the perfect succession of Ws; the first stain on a new carpet.

Nine months and six wins later, Pring and I were together under the roof of Colston Hall once again. But not before two genuine delays, which were seized upon and misshapen by the press. First I suffered a severe cut and then, with the fight rearranged and impending, I woke up a couple of days before shivering and sweating. I had two fevers to lose: influenza and Joe Pring. As the flu weakened my body, Pring haunted my mind. My father came to my sickbed, the harbinger of bad news. "They say you're yellow, son. They say you're faking because you're scared of him." As if I hadn't proved myself in eleven other fights. This coalman was like a mark upon me, the way a champion is never a true champion when the crown is vacated through a technicality.

The psychological game can go one of two ways: it can make a man unsure of himself, because there is always fear with the relative equality of two fighters, or it can galvanize determination. Because of all the talk I wanted to hurt Pring, which may seem the transparent requirement for a boxer and yet his aim is never figured in such terms. A coach might say "Watch how he drops his left when he jabs with the right, there's the chance." The talented and successful boxer will exploit this, knowing that this is the opportunity for another point, another crunch of the brain. Yet the desire to inflict pain is wayward and the boxer who is motivated by it will always be found out.

However, nothing is sacred in something as unreasonable as boxing and my second fight against Pring was all over in twenty seconds. He was prostrate on the canvas after ten and then there was the count. No man goes down that quick unless he's been truly hurt or he's terrible at throwing punches. Now I don't claim to have ended Joe Pring's professional career, but I did hear, from those same raconteurs who had riled me, that he never laced-up his gloves again.

After the double beating of Randall and before Pring, I had left the army. My two years were up and I could concentrate all my efforts on boxing. The first thing was to try and rectify my poor training regime. Luckily around this time a man I knew from the fairground, Pat McKeown, who ran a boxing booth had brought his mobile ring to the Maltsters Arms in Exeter for the off-season. It was there I attended the first regular gym of my professional career, it was unorthodox but helped establish a routine. I used it to prepare for my fight against a Welshman, Terry Edwards, that was bookended by the last Randall and the first Pring fight. Edwards had been undefeated in twelve prior to our match-up and came with a fearsome reputation. I remember the promotional posters tried to engender something of the Wild West in the tagline, calling it the 'West Country Vs Wales Showdown'. Not quite 'the fight of the century' but I thought it cute that my bouts were now important enough to by backed by a primitive marketing campaign.

Whilst training at Pat McKeown's booth, the proximity of a pub meant that most days we would end up perched on stools with a packet of crisps and a pint. I would order a light ale and supped half of it whilst Pat and his wife waited for their black stout to

PAUL KING (Torquay)
Young King became a professional last summer after a splendid career as an amateur. He had his first professional fight at Plymouth on a Freddie Lawson – George Harrison bill and since then he has gone from strength to strength. He has yet to be beaten, and with his boxing ability allied with his first-rate punching, he is beginning to look like a potential threat to the best welters in the country.

A GEORGE HARRISON PRESENTATION

GREAT "NEEDLE" INTERNATIONAL MATCH
West of England v. Wales

SIX ROUNDS WELTERWEIGHT
PAUL KING v. TERRY EDWARDS
(TORQUAY)   (PORT TALBOT)
ALL ROUNDS OF THREE-MINUTES' DURATION

settle. They would look at my glass with the disapproval of the connoisseur, call me a philistine. They pointed to a poster on the pub wall that had a picture of a country man who had swapped roles with his horse. Above the image, in large red capital letters it stated: Guinness for Strength. So I tried a pint of Guinness and I liked it.

It was due to this that when I got on the scales for the weigh-in for the Edwards bout, I found I was overweight. I was told I'd have to lose the weight or forfeit five pounds sterling. Because I partly blamed him, Pat concocted a plan to redeem himself. He said that I should forfeit the money, then he would bet a little extra on me, enough to raise five more pounds, and give me what I had forfeited back. I'd already listened to him once and he'd made me fat, but I had no other option. Losing the weight was unrealistic in the small amount of time remaining before the fight. For all this to work, I'd have to knock Edwards out. The bet wouldn't work on a points decision or a technical knock out.

The first two rounds were scored one each, his the first, mine the second. But I felt that I'd hurt him much more than he'd hurt me and anyway, he'd bettered me and I'd come back. It was up to him to reply, I had the momentum now. In the third I caught him a left jab on the nose and he reeled, clumsily treading backwards, blindly reversing, arms flailing in no defence at all. I wrapped a vicious right hook round his head to send him down and there he stayed, out cold. I was jubilant and so was Pat; the five pounds was restored and we went back to the Maltsters Arms where he bought me a congratulatory Guinness.

CHAPTER 7

THE COLONEL

Soon after the first fight with Pring, a friend of mine, Eddie, called me up and said he'd met someone I might be interested in. Eddie's connection with boxing was no greater than his being a spectator when money and time allowed, and an eager ear for sporting news when it didn't. The job that prevented him from watching as many fights as he would have liked was as the Maître d' of the Edenhurst Hotel in Torquay. It was there that he'd shared an interesting conversation on boxing with one of the more eccentric guests; a Colonel who followed the sport and proclaimed himself to be on intimate terms with Len Harvey. The Colonel had told Eddie that he had heard of a Torbay boxer called Paul King, who was making himself known by his refusal to be bettered in the ring. Eddie had mentioned that he too had friends in the boxing world and that I was one of them. The Colonel had been filled with enthusiasm and said that he must meet me. Consequently Eddie had phoned to invite me, on behalf of the Colonel, to dinner at the Edenhurst. In my world dinner was something that was eaten in the middle of the day and so I told Eddie that I wouldn't be able to make it as I still had my job at the refrigeration engineers. Eddie admonished my innocence "Paul, you are yokel, aren't you? He means in the evening, dinner is the evening meal." So I set a date.

I pressed my best shirt in deference to this man I imagined as having standards that needed to be met; who else could pluck someone who interested him from out of the mass and compel them to dine with him? I wondered whether it would prove to be of any benefit to me, or whether I was merely going to engage the whim of a crackpot old man. I couldn't help but speculate, I even

EDENHURST PRIVATE HOTEL TORQUAY

A most Comfortable Hotel in which to spend the Autumn and Winter, because of its magnificent position and perfect quietude ; within 3 minutes of the Shopping Centre, Medical Baths, Pier, Pavilion and Theatres. From its lawns and terraces (over 150 feet long), one of the most glorious views in England is obtained.

PERFECT SERVICE : HOT AND COLD WATER THROUGHOUT : GARAGE ADJOINING

thought, what if he's a poof? However I decided to stay loyal to Eddie and the free meal, thinking I could box my way out if necessary.

The reception area at the Edenhurst was vast. I happened to walk in when the front desk wasn't manned and the room was empty. I rang the bell and the noise rose sharply. It sounded demanding and I didn't feel that I should be demanding in such a place. Soft footsteps padded along the carpet of the corridor, betrayed by their rhythmical polished squeak. A man with a tight suit and a scarlet face appeared. "Hello, can I be of some assistance?" I had expected a receptionist or someone who worked at the hotel, but he obviously didn't work there. I told him that I was looking for a Colonel Forsyth. He replied, with a long, smooth "Ahhh" and continued "So you must be Paul King" To me he looked as much like a Colonel as he did a receptionist. I smiled and told him I was. He reached forward and I shook his hand. "Then come with me, Paul, please."

This was my first impression of Eric, that he looked neither like a hotel receptionist or a colonel. What he was, in fact, was the Colonel's personal valet, a 'gentleman's gentleman' as he liked to put it. When we arrived at the Colonel's room, Eric told me that the man himself was just finishing his bath and he offered me a drink, gesturing towards the drinks cabinet. I was astounded. An array of liquor bottles sparkled in front of me. I mumbled something about a light ale. Eric poured a clear liquid from one of the bottles and topped it with carbonated water; I took it and thanked him, not wanting to embarrass myself further by asking what it was. I took a sip and had to tense my jaw so as not to grimace from the taste. I learned that it was a gin and tonic and also that Eric drank a lot of gin.

Then he appeared, the Colonel himself, shaved bone-close, his thinning coiffure immaculate, a continental odour wafting around him, wearing a thin robe that I thought must be pure silk. "Good evening, Paul, so good of you to come," he said with an elegance that was bred and taught so young that it was as natural as my own awkwardness. Immediately he joined myself and Eric with a drink, pouring a large measure of golden whisky into a glass: four fingers. An amount I learned, he could hit with the exactness of a veteran French sommelier, by sight alone.

He introduced himself and spoke of his interest in boxing, mentioning his friendship with Len Harvey but revealing little of himself. Then he began asking me about myself, about my fights so far and my technique. He told me that he marvelled at the ability of a man to climb into a confined space with another man and to sacrifice his physical integrity in the name of sport, to subjugate that man to pain in order to win. "For there must be a winner," he said with a smile. "There is something desperate about violence, the clamour for life; the realisation that living is enough in itself and there need not be some dreary notion of meaning beyond that. Do you not think so, Paul?" This type of conversation certainly wasn't anything I was used to and I found myself just agreeing.

The important facts about the Colonel I found out later, incrementally. Lieutenant-Colonel Frederick Richard Gerard Forsyth MC, DL, was born in Netherleigh, Leamington in 1882. The military ran in his family; his father was a Lieutenant-Colonel of the 5th Fusiliers. As a teenager he had joined the Seaforth Highlanders, fought in the Boer War in 1901-2, where he was injured in a derailment of the no. 12 armoured train and was awarded a medal and five clasps. He earned a medal and a clasp on the north-west frontier in India and the Royal Humane Bronze Medal for saving the life of a fellow soldier in 1905. He was made a Captain in 1914 at the outbreak of the Great War, before transferring to the 4th (RI) Dragoon Guards at the same rank. He managed to avoid the premature death that was the fate of half the other men of his generation, but was wounded three times, he was twice mentioned in dispatches. After the First World War he moved to the newly formed Royal Signal Corps and in 1926 was honoured with the title that I knew him by. For this detailed military biography I am indebted to his gentleman, Eric, for like many soldiers who have seen combat, the Colonel was never too free with his war memories, thinking it a sign of vulgarity to flaunt such achievements.

This, however, he did tell me himself, showing me the primary evidence with bombast. He was considered significant enough to be included in that prestigious chronicler of the biographies of the privileged and the talented: _Who's Who_. His entry told that he was a member of the Cavalry and Ocean Racing clubs and that his recreational activities included racing, steeplechasing, yachting, shooting and fishing. His friends knew him by the sobriquet 'Chaser', owing to his _Who's Who_ days as a gentleman jockey and his continuing connections with the turf. Something else he wasn't quiet about was his boozing. Of his many talents I often thought that this was possibly his greatest. He drank unrivalled amounts of whisky, whilst Eric did the same for gin, which no doubt was as it should have been and a class thing.

Dinner was served on a large platter by room service. The Colonel explained that he didn't eat much in the evenings as he found it was bad for his circulation. Then, pouring another whisky, he told me that he was very fond of travelling, but had recently spent a good stretch in the West Country. He had noticed the frequent appearance of my name in the local papers, lauding me as a local hero. As I laid a piece of cold ham on a large slice of bread smeared with paté, he eyed me and said he thought he may be able to assist me in some way.

I left the Colonel and Eric with a promise from them that they would be in touch. Semi-inebriation made his assertion a pleasant surrealism, like the unexpected interest of a wealthy patron for a poverty stricken artist. The next morning it all seemed very strange and I regretted my subordination, wishing that I'd asked more questions. Nevertheless the Colonel and Eric had managed to find out where I was training and turned up the next week at the hall in Upton Vale. I was ashamed then and I am ashamed now, but for different reasons. The hall was in a desperate condition, with hardly a brushstroke of paint attached to the wall and broken windows that had felt the frustration of local youths. I was ashamed and my heart leapt in bashfulness, thinking that the Colonel and Eric in their long expensive overcoats, would view it with condescension from the edge of the hall. Now I am ashamed I ever had such snobbish aspirations.

I tried to counter the destitution of the venue by shadow boxing lightly and with restraint, skipping consistently and hitting the bag with such persuasive force that they would forget where they were and be engrossed by my performance. After getting to know the Colonel I realised that I had misinterpreted his display at the

Edenhurst and out of my own personal fear and ignorance, I had cruelly stereotyped an unconventional individual. When I finished he clapped loudly with ostentation and proclaimed "Bravo, bravo, Paul! I think we'd better give Mr Harvey a ring and get him to talk to you, eh?"

CHAPTER 8

LEN HARVEY

If I was intimidated by the Colonel, then having to speak to Len Harvey was likely to lay me down dead. I had watched the Pathé newsreel of his final fight with Freddie Mills during the war, when he finished with a whimper after so many glorious bangs, feeling the sadness because a beacon of old grace had been put out by youth and angry strength. But the past could not be diminished by those four short minutes. Harvey's achievements, if piled end on end, would have reached heaven. Not only in his style, but also in his manner. He was exemplary; an anathema to all those who browbeat the sport, not because he was what they purported to hate, but because he gave physical and mental realisation to all the values that they said were incompatible with boxing. Reg Gutteridge, that dean of boxing commentary said it best: "If the maligned business of prize fighting could have produced a knight, Len Harvey would have been the traders' choice. Scrape the bottom of boxing's rumour-ridden barrel and you will never hear a bad word about him."

Harvey claimed to have fought four hundred and fourteen bouts in his career, and to have won at least four hundred of those. In the days before the pound for pound rating, Harvey attempted to prove he was the best, by boxing in every weight division from fly to heavy. A list of his titles, challenges and defences is like a train with a never-ending line of carriages. His first attempt was for the British welterweight title, but the fight was a draw. Then in 1929, he won the British and Empire middleweight titles and defended them for four years whilst also challenging and failing to get the World middleweight. Immediately after losing the middleweight title he took the vacant British light-heavyweight crown, before

upgrading and taking the British heavyweight and Empire titles, both at the Royal Albert Hall in front of ten thousand. And all of this in 1933. The next year he lost both of these titles to the old champ, Jack Petersen, this time with ninety thousand hot-blooded pugilist freaks baying at the White City Stadium. However, this didn't stop him from bringing John Henry Lewis to Wembley for a World light-heavyweight fight in 1936. Harvey took the American to fifteen full rounds, but damaged his hand and could only desperately open an old cut from training on Lewis, who took the points decision.

Soon however, Harvey won his old titles back again, first the British heavyweight, against his former middleweight nemesis Jock McAvoy, and then the Empire, both of which had been vacated by the Tonypandy Terror in preparation for his fateful Madison Square Gardens bout with Joe Louis. Just before the war Harvey had dropped down a division to light-heavyweight, without being defeated for his heavyweight titles, and beaten McAvoy once more for both the British and Empire crowns. The British boxing authorities also regarded this as a fight to decide the vacant World light-heavyweight title athough it was not universally sanctified. Finally, there was the bout that I remembered from the Pathé reels, which was a defence of the two undisputed light-heavy-weight titles he held.

The fight against Freddie Mills was in 1942 in the middle of the war. Previous to this, the last time Harvey had boxed was his bout with McAvoy before the war. Since then he'd joined the RAF, his fame had achieved him a commission and a position as a physical training instructor. Mills had been fighting through the elimination rounds to get his chance at the title; also defeating McAvoy. Still, Harvey needed persuading, but those who knew how managed it, no doubt playing on his conscience by calling it part of the war effort; a more palatable form of violence to divert the public. And so the venue, White Hart Lane, was prepared.

In the stands and on the football field at the Spurs' stadium forty thousand people jostled for a view as the news cameras were recording. Mills was fresh, he'd been fighting bouts regularly. Harvey was fit but his toughness had regressed. Their styles were different cultures: Harvey had verve and brains, he'd gyrate in odd whirls as the other mans fists touched nothing but air, or he'd form an impenetrable phalanx with his great forearms and then toss his arm like a war spear at the other mans face. He was the epitome of boxers who use artifice over rough force. Mills was such a rough force, a man of one punch, though he seemed to have several chins. He could take extraordinary punishment and all the while propel his fists in identical motion at his victim. Their statures seemed to reflect this: Mills was shorter with tight, curly hair; Harvey was tall and geometric. In testament to his defensive abilities, his face looked as if the most dangerous place it had ever been in was a book.

At White Hart Lane Mills felled Harvey's defence pretty quickly. In the first round Harvey was quicker, jabbing Mills, then drawing back and to the side to avoid the inevitable untamed charge. I always remember one massive left hook that had Mills pouncing forwards in a four pointed star jump and Harvey side-stepping faster than light, Mills obviously still able to see his image though he was longer there. Then Harvey would try to contain him and subdue him in clinches and there would be infighting. In the second it was over almost immediately. Harvey lunged clumsily with a left and opened a huge hole in front of his face, as Mills took the punch he breached Harvey and sent him down. The referee counted to nine with Harvey pulling on the ropes to stand. Then Mills advanced and Harvey tried a last desperate clinch, but Mills rammed his body like he was doing bag work and broke free. Harvey staggered backwards and was caught by the ropes; he bent into an arch and wavered up and down and up and down. Mills raged on and gave the significant left. All Harvey's weight rested on the second rope, which bulged towards the canvas. Momentarily he sat perfectly upright as though taking tea and then he was lost beyond the ring. The referee looked like a man trying to swat a bug, no-one but those in the closest ringside seats could see Harvey now. It was a sad end for a glorious fighter, but what memories. After the war he did what all intelligent sportsmen do and became licensed. He was landlord of a series of pubs, of which The Star and Garter in Islington was the most prestigious.

I was unsure if the Colonel was playing some sort of game, but he insisted that I accompany him and Eric directly to the Edenhurst and become acquainted with Harvey that very night. I sat in their hotel room as Eric fused more gin with tonic for me and the Colonel dialled the telephone from memory. "Ah, Len, Chaser here. How are you, old man? And Blossom? Ever spring of course. Excellent. Look here, I've got this boy with me now, Paul King. Very promising. Have a word with him for me will you?" I noticed that he mentioned nothing of me being a boxer. I felt Harvey must have been primed, as if the phone call was mere show and everything had been arranged beforehand in the presumption that I would be compliant.

The Colonel passed me the telephone. I was still incredulous and could feel the muscles on the back of my neck undergoing multitudes of tiny convulsions. "He-hello, Mr Harvey?" I stammered, turning the greeting into a question. "Yes; is that, Paul? Hello, Paul! So, Chaser tells me you've a formidable record to your name?" "Err... Yes, well, yes." "Well, I'd very much like meet you, Paul. There's a fight coming up, Randolf Turpin and Walter Cartier, it's at Earls Court. I have some tickets if you'd like to come along?" "Yes, yes, that would be – " "Perfect! If you come up with the Colonel and Eric, we'll meet at my pub and have a lubricator or two before we go." "Yes. I mean, thank you, Mr Harvey." "Great. Put Chaser back on, will you?"

Walking home I didn't have a clue whether I'd spoken to Len Harvey or some impersonator who had been given a script and paid to sit by a phone all evening. Not that I had any reason to suspect the Colonel, but Len Harvey! In my mind the name rolled continuously in a tone of disbelief. I thought to myself that if it was true, then it was too good to be true and must be worth a chance.

I doubt I would be writing this were it not true. I subsequently travelled up to London with the Colonel and Eric and we met Len Harvey at his pub. He proceeded to pour us each a drink over greetings, after which we took a taxi to Earls Court. The instance that still remains the most significant for me, was when we tried to enter the venue. At the gate Harvey told the steward who he was and received a dismissive "Yeah, we've had six of you already." I was incredulous at the steward's ignorance and was about to give it voice, but Harvey, unfazed, told me not to worry and that someone would recognise him soon enough. Sure enough someone soon did and the steward squirmed under his mistake. Not that Harvey was bitter, he gave him a wink and said "You'll know me next time eh?" His lack of need to assert his status really impressed me. I felt that not many people, given his position, would have been so forgiving.

As for the fight, it was simply strange. Cartier fought as though scared of Turpin. There was only a sparse collection of punches that even connected; all from Turpin. Cartier seemed to have a contrary devil inside him, for he continued to hold Turpin's arms even though the referee continuously warned him. By the second round he'd had enough and disqualified the American, holding Turpin's arm aloft. What happened after became more of a fight than the bout itself. I suppose they had to provide some entertainment in reparation for Cartier's ugly mood. His camp clambered into the ring to barrack the referee, joining the boxer himself in his show of acrimony. If Cartier was a justly castrated bull, then Turpin was a confused sheep dog. It was not much of a win and the crowd was too engrossed in the American side show to congratulate him, he just joined those trying to shield the referee. Then recognising the pettiness of it all, he stood bemused in the middle of the ring, awkward and redundant. Cartier and his crowd were an enemy of their own sport. The type of men that the public, ignorant of the boxing fraternity and with no imagination, would assume were typical.

Len Harvey was the opposite. His body was densely packed and roughly hewn yet his voice was as mild as an early summer's evening. He had the disconcerting habit of staring directly at you when he spoke, as if the confrontation of the ring had seeped into his personality. He lacked the effusive regard for his own voice that many retired fighters have, with their love for their own anecdote and memory. Len's reserve imitated his coy boxing tactics. The public loved him, his status and past achievements always held them in awe. He drank from the generosity of others and as a result his wallet remained firmly out of sight. Len had only those little troubles that afflict every man, nothing too large to deal with. He had his pubs and his wife Florence, 'Blossom' to him, who had told him on their first meeting "Go and find the real Len Harvey, I might go out with him, but not you" and who loved him until death. She was ubiquitous wherever Len was and had ever been, even when he was boxing. And he was unimpressed by any trainer who frowned upon it.

A late night followed the Turpin/Cartier fight at The Derby Arms, the whisky and gin bottles behind Len's bar soon had to be replaced. All that came from the meeting with Harvey was a verification of the Colonel's references: he was who he said he was. Nothing was agreed upon. Nothing as to how the Colonel and Harvey might help me. So I went away with a sense of having wealthy and powerful friends, but little that was certain.

Left to right: The Colonel, Eric and Len Harvey

CHAPTER 9

TOP OF THE BILL

After sharing a bar with one of boxing's aristocracy, going to work again at the refrigeration company was like climbing out of a warm bath into a snow storm. Even though I was professional, I was still working during the day and training most nights. The career of a professional sportsman can easily be destabilised. Injuries, especially in boxing, are always a risk, inexplicable cuts filling your eyes with blood are always an emasculating way to lose. Talk to failed boxers and it was always an injustice, or you simply find that those who told you that you were good enough, never had the authority to do so in the first place. That was why Jack Turner, Taff, all the old pros I knew and my mother had convinced me to keep my unwanted job at the refrigeration company, because, she said, the prudent man will never go hungry.

But my focus was boxing. My first fight after meeting Len and the Colonel was against Pat Gamble, who had been boxing professionally since 1937, the year of the Louis/Farr title fight. I was Pat's penultimate bout. Not that he wasn't still able; he'd won his previous two fights, but he'd spent his entire professional career in the town halls and corn exchanges of the West Country. To denigrate any boxer is beyond me, but preparing for the bout, I knew that his was the type of career that would necessitate having a job to return to at its conclusion. It was like fighting fate. To win would assert my will to form my own career, to be beaten would prove my cautious elders to be prescient. In my mind, those were the stakes I placed on the Pat Gamble fight. When it came to it I had no trouble. Pat hit the canvas more times than I can remember and the referee stopped it in the fifth round and gave me the win.

This was eight fights and seven wins and the promoters at the Winter Gardens Pavilion in Weston-super-Mare thought that such a record could suckle the crowd well enough to top the bill. Quite an honour the first time you do it. My placing attracted at least two extra spectators; the Colonel and Eric were to be there for the first time. The poster, I still have a copy, had mine and Mick Angell's names emblazoned across the middle in large red letters and underneath, a little prose for the connoisseurs; detail for the gamblers. Mine read: 'Unbeaten to date. Brilliant ex-amateur record. First time here. A real up and coming youngster and number one contender for area title honours'. Mick Angell, of Cricklewood, was a furious boxer. Another coalman, he had knocked out my only blemish, Joe Pring. Angell had beaten Pring, I had only drawn with him.

Rising to the top of the bill had its duties; you weren't simply the top attraction. Headliners of variety shows were always given the longest time on stage and those principles of entertainment were no different in the boxing world. This meant that, unless one of us could knock the other out before, we would go for eight rounds. I felt that my untamed style, which did not know how to slow down for a regenerative pause, would not compliment extra rounds. There had been a couple of fights already that had gone to a points decision and where I felt that any more time in the ring might have meant my defeat. I should have learned how to extend myself over longer periods, but boxing isn't something you can learn from a book. Although I was a professional, my training set-up was amateur. This is where I thought that the Colonel and Len Harvey might help. But for the immediacy of the Angell fight, I had to go with what I knew.

After the fight I thought with ever more certainty that the Pring anomaly was due to the debilitating effect of nerves. My fight with Angell had reached the full eight rounds. The punters had seen all they paid for and I discovered that Angell's profile on the poster, which had described him as 'all-action', had really meant that he

WINTER GARDENS PAVILION

Director of Entertainments : I. DAVIES　　*Pavilion Manager : D. S. ASHMAN*

WESTON-SUPER-MARE

— Monday, 28th July, 1952 at 7.30 p.m. —

The Weston-super-Mare Sportsmen's Organisation (B.B.B. of C.) present a

Grand Professional Boxing Tournament

Terrific 6 3-min. rds. Middleweight Contest at 11-st.2-lbs.

DON DESBOROUGH　v.　JOHNNY MUDGE

Hanwell.　　　　　　　　　　　　**Torquay.**
Grand tough two-handed battler.　　All-round fighter and great crowd pleaser

Great Special Attraction - 8 3-min. rds. Welterweight Contest at 10-st. 8-lbs.

PAUL KING

TORQUAY. Unbeaten to date. Brilliant ex-amateur record. First time here.
A real up-and-coming youngster and No. 1 contender for area title honours.

v.

MICK ANGELL

CRICKLEWOOD. Beaten Ken Tizor, Arthur Garratt, Johnny Godfrey, Ronnie
Moore, Fred Morris, Benny Leonard, Johnny Joackson, and on his last appearance
here K.O.d. Joe Pring. Good all-action fighter. Don't miss this fistic treat.

Special 6 3-mins. rds. Featherweight Contest at 9-st.5-lbs.

Harry RAMSDEN　v.　Brian GOODWIN

R.A.F. Hereford. Unbeaten to date.　**Fulham.** Tough all-action Boy.
Nice classy boxer.　　　　　　　　　Won 5. Lost 1.

was suffering from the same problem as myself. I wish it had been filmed, for the fury that the crowd must have enjoyed is a real rarity in boxing. We were two fighters who didn't know how to let up. But the pivot on which the fight revolved was a queer occurrence indeed. Angell had a move where, at the beginning of every round, he would dodge backwards and grapple me in a clinch and then whisper something in my ear. But he was so softly spoken that, ludicrously, I couldn't hear a word. Then he would step back and glare at me, as if to reinforce his words. I was completely nonplussed; the only chance he had of gaining any advantage from it would be to befuddle his opponent into thinking that he was clinically insane. At the beginning of the sixth round, as he was trying to whisper his sweet nothings I couldn't help but laugh at this weird tactic. He was evidently shocked and bristled backwards. Immediately I rammed several right-hooks to the left side of his face. He crumpled in hurt and there was an audible collective rush of shock from the crowd. It must have looked like he was trying to throw the fight because his guard had dropped completely. From the beginning of the sixth I had the fight. He didn't try his whispering clinch in the seventh or eighth and the decision was firmly mine. The Colonel and Eric congratulated me with a drink in the changing room, they said they liked what they saw and that they knew some good pubs in Weston-super-Mare.

Fights just seemed to roll like loosened rocks in a landslide in the late summer of 1952. Next up was Morrie Gibny, who was a bred Scot, whereas I was just a born Scot. Bred out of Torquay I took my moniker from the town and was baptised in the corner of the ring with a bucket of water as the 'Torquay Tornado'. The *nom-de-boxe* came from all the supporters I was capturing back in my home town, but it was to be a while until I fought in a homecoming bout. The local aficionados were passing the word around and the more wins I tallied, the more Torbay natives would travel around the West Country every time I boxed. They made it all the way to Portsmouth to watch me force the referee to stop the Gibny fight in the second round.

After that it was my turn to serve the people of Devon. A biblical storm had erupted over the towns of Lynmouth and Linton that summer. Floods ripped through the landscape and many people died and were injured. In response Freddie Mills, the philanthropist, had organised a night of charity boxing at Barnstaple Market Hall, from which all proceeds would go to the disaster fund. The most exotic man I had boxed up until then had been the Glaswegian, Gibny, so when I was paired with Jack Kofi from the Gold Coast, I took it as a sign that my career might just move out of the provinces. Not that Jack Kofi was any great fighter, in fact he was exactly the opposite. He would never excite any promoters; he was not a contender of any kind. And I was fighting him in Barnstaple! But the naked facts never seemed to matter much in boxing.

The Torquay Tornado fans, of which there were many that night, had chartered a coach. My father even managed to give his taxi a night off from the town roads and let it see some countryside. There was a slight mishap in the changing room beforehand when I realised my proud new robe was actually a dressing gown and I couldn't fit my gloves down the sleeves. Unfortunately I had to go into the ring bare-chested. Kofi was insatiable for punishment and kept coming until the end, even though I cut him badly above the eye and on the lip. Sometimes it is fortune that makes a boxer bleed, but when a body drips with blood and sweat on the floor from two lacerations, unless he's dripping on the other man's body, he has surely lost the fight.

And so, after Kofi, came my last fight of the summer, before my rematch with Joe Pring. I confess that some of my professional bouts are locked in my unreachable memory. Perhaps one day, a name or someone with the narrative at easy recall will remind me, but until then all I have are the basics of the night. Maybe it was my consistent return to the Connaught Drill Hall in Portsmouth that causes my lack of memory; this was the third and last time. But enough is to be said about the Hugh O'Donnell fight – I won.

What followed was a seemingly interminable delay, caused by my own cuts and illness, that forestalled the second match-up with Pring until the autumn. Post-Pring my record read twelve wins and one draw. It was then that I was booked to fight outside the South West for the first time. Myself and Eric Skidmore were both dispatched to Preston to box second on the bill to one of Jack Turner's stable boys Teddy Peckham. Skidmore was up for the Midlands' area title against Mosh Mancini, which he subsequently won.. Despite this, I had him down for counts in the first, fifth and last rounds and was given the points decision. There I was, travelling up north, my first fight in an unfamiliar area and beating the Midlands' area welterweight champion to be. Not that I expected a single night in Preston to remove the need to learn a trade, but it did prompt Jack Turner to deluge me with letters encouraging me to move to Bournemouth and train with him full time, which meant giving up my job in the refrigeration factory.

At this point it seemed to me that what I most wanted was coming. I deliberated for two more fights, beating Noel Sinfield in three rounds and then Bobby Johnson on points;.two more wins. The Colonel accused me of prevaricating. He told me that I couldn't keep on winning and stay in Torquay because sooner or later someone would come and drag me out. A winner was worth money and more. Len Harvey thought that the only place to go was the capital, where everything took off. But I knew that this wasn't entirely true and that some things could be swallowed by its magnitude. Nevertheless, a decision had to be taken.

BOXING

TOWN HALL, CHELTENHAM   7.45 p.m.   Doors open 7 p.m.

MONDAY, 2nd FEBRUARY, 1953

Promoted by the Cheltenham Corporation.   Matchmaker : JACK KING.   Licensed by the B.B.B. of C. (1929)

GREAT ALL-STAR ACTION PROGRAMME

Great Middleweight Attraction.   Special Eight (3 min.) Rounds Contest at 11 st. 8 lbs.

EDDIE WEBB

JAMAICA'S tough all action fighter.   Record—Bobby Fish, Ken Whitty, Bob Cleaver, etc.

v.

JIMMY REDGWELL

ASHFORD.   Record includes Ron Cook, Sammy Millson, Michael Stack, Johnny Wright, George Roe, Bob Cleaver, etc.
Weigh-in at Town Hall on day of contest at 1 p.m.

Great Six (3 min.) Rounds Middleweight Contest at 11 st. 8 lbs.	All action Six (3 min.) Rounds Featherweight Contest at 9 st. 4 lbs.
ROGER CORBETT	**BILLY DANIELS**
Gloucester v.	Bow v.
KEN MULLINS	**PAT McCOY**
Jamaica.	Ireland.
Six (2 min.) Rounds Contest at 9 st. 4 lbs.	Six (2 min.) Rounds Welterweight Contest at 10 st. 7 lbs.
JOHNNY WILLIAMSON	**KEN SCAMMELL**
Gloucester v.	Wandsworth v.
TERRY LUMSDEN	**ARTHUR ROGERS**
Bristol.	Gloucester.

Important Welterweight Attraction.   Grand Eight (3 min.) Rounds Contest at 10 st. 7 lbs.

PAUL KING

TORQUAY.   Contender for area title.   Unbeaten to date.   Great prospect.

v.

NOEL SINFIELD

BARNSLEY.   Record—Johnny Pipe, Mick Angell, Bernie Newcombe, Alf Lay, Harry Warner, etc.

ADMISSION :   5/6 ;   11/6 ;   17/6 ;   25/-   (including tax)

Booking and Tickets from Town Hall, Cheltenham (Tel. 2200) ;   Messrs. Hickie and Hickie, Southgate Street, Gloucester (Tel. 21061) ; Bishop's, Newsagents, 270 High Street, Cheltenham. (Tel. 53626).

Applications for Tickets by Post should be accompanied by remittance and stamped addressed envelope. Cheques and Postal Orders payable to Cheltenham Corporation.

NOTE —All tickets reserved must be claimed and paid for before the day of the show, otherwise they will be sold.

Norman, Sawyer & Co. Ltd., St. George's Street, Cheltenham.

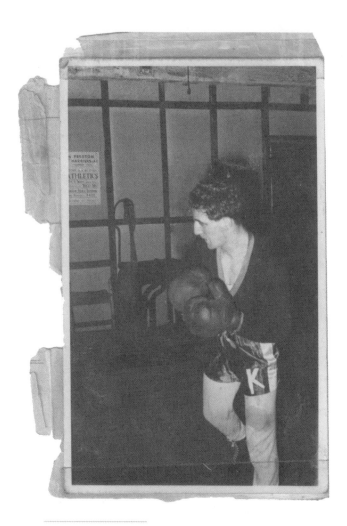

Training in Preston, 1953

CHAPTER 10

BOURNEMOUTH BLUES

Len Harvey had said, 'come to London', but there was no plan, no manager, no trainer, no gym, nothing organised. Jack Turner, despite all his shortcomings, was experienced. He had a record with world beating fighters and he had organised all my fights so far. Not that I felt I owed him anything, he was as ruthless as any animal, but his proposition was the most business-like option I had. He had promised five pounds a week, an excellent gym and quality fighters to spar with. So when I turned up at the door of a town house, encased between two shops, it was in Upper Parkstone, Bournemouth and not East Sheen, London.

Jack Turner was drunk. "Whaddaryoudoin'ere?" He stuttered from his permanently rouged visage with swivelling bloodshot eye. I forced my way in through the door and eventually made him realise, through his stupor, that I had turned up to box. "Well, you're not staying 'ere." And so we walked around Parkstone, a dour place, seeking lodgings. Jack abused a few spinsters and widows and finally, miraculously, he secured me a room in a house that could be reviled only on a par with smallpox. There were four of us sleeping in one room with no heating. The other lodgers were a group of Irish labourers, who worked under exploitation and relieved themselves through alcoholic weekends. They often fought each other and would constantly rib me, asking for boxing lessons. I always told them that boxing had too many rules for them. If I had fought them, they would have ripped my balls off.

If I didn't get down for breakfast as soon as it was laid on the table they would eat mine for me; if I took too long eating it they would snatch the sausages from my plate and thank me. This was all done with such childlike ignorance that it would have been self-defeating to argue. One particularly raucous Saturday night they put a chair leg through the bedroom window and then patched it with cardboard. They would change it when it had soaked up enough rainwater to cause it to sag. The appearance of the land-lady's daughter engendered whistles and cat-calls, which always maddened her husband into lazy Irish slurs, the irony of which made it impossible for them to take offence. Instead they would pat him on the shoulder and take his sausages. I liked them then because I hated her husband with a mixture of jealousy and disgust.

During the first few weeks in Bournemouth all I did was go to the gym, do my road work, sleep and sit in cafés. At times I felt a fool for ever leaving Torquay, It was as if I was somewhere I wasn't wanted, a place that could never accept me. Whenever I was out of the gym I felt meek and supplicant, as if the people of Bournemouth knew I was an interloper and scorned me as such. Jack was no help; when the landlady asked for the weekly rent I had to give her my booth money (Jack still got me gigs at the fair-ground most weekends), because my promised professional weekly wage, for the first month, was absent. I had left Torquay and quit my job with just seventeen pounds in the bank and even that was beginning to dwindle. When I confronted Jack he would merely harp about the booth money and ask me if I could do without that too. He was a manipulator, a true spieler who found it easy to distract the conversation away from subjects uncomfortable for him.

Several times in the first few weeks I nearly retreated back along the coast. But apart from the wish to advance my boxing career, I had another more ignoble motivation willing me to stay. My father had never liked Jack Turner, he called him a charlatan and a show-off. When I moved he wouldn't say goodbye because he said he knew I'd soon be back. It would have raised all the bile from my stomach to return a failure and see him bathe in his pool of bitter pessimism, goading me to join him. For the avoidance of this scene, I knew I couldn't go back.

Despite this psychological malady, I only had reason to be optimistic. My departure from Torquay had been heralded by the local newspaper, and had been very flattering. At least now I had full time training, if not the wage, and the use of facilities and coaching to maintain my unbeaten run. The first bout Jack organised for me whilst I was in Bournemouth, necessitated a repeat visit to Preston public hall. This time I was to fight Peter Smith; the first of a triple header against the Huddersfield man. The way it fell into place, I would be his opponent for the next three times he was in the ring. It was something of a relief that the fight was to take place in Preston as it gave me several days away from the crumbling den in Bournemouth that I thought must have been like life in a Victorian slum. Jack at least knew the value of presentation; before travelling to Preston he sent me to his tailor and I was measured for a new suit. He said that the suit was my wage; so I grabbed a trilby hat and added that to the bill to ensure he paid me in full. When I arrived at the hall in Lancashire I was approached by a man who enquired if I was Paul King. I was surprised and asked him how he knew. He said Jack Turner had told him to look out for 'a flash bastard'.

That night I pedalled my usual unsophisticated rampage which up to now had been so successful. I was at last training in the right way, but it had almost come too late. I felt scared to abandon the techniques that had taken me through sixteen fights unbeaten. Smith looked awkward as he attempted to evade my punches, backtracking, and throw piston-like jabs as though he was a steam train reversing across the canvas. It was almost as if he didn't think that he could knock me out and was aiming to win on points. There was something mathematical about the way Smith fought that was entirely alien to me. Perhaps there simply wasn't enough time in the eight rounds for his technique to fully flourish. The next day the newspapers called it a close result and it may have looked it, but I never felt that he was doing enough. That was my sixteenth win, seventeen unbeaten.

On the road and in the ring I had forgotten my Irish boys, but they hadn't forgotten me and told me they were pleased I was back because they'd been missing their extra sausages. The distance between us and the time apart, had made me realise that it simply wasn't working and I needed a new place to stay. Not that I actively sought somewhere, it was merely a wish. Then, one day on my walk back from training, passing the Post Office I noticed a card propped in the window that said: 'Full board. Own room. Two Shillings a week.' I rang the number that night and arranged to go and see the place. Though I didn't know it yet, this was the revolution of a new cycle.

The woman who answered the door was beautiful as a piece of architecture, the way that old buildings are often more desirable than new ones. She was attentive and nervous like a junior sales-man, but my old lodgings had done the work for her. The place was clean, tidy and private, the living room had no television but instead a radio. She and her husband obviously cared about where they lived, and to me it was as homely as I had ever had. As she smiled and told me that they were 'just ordinary people', I almost cried in praise of prosaic and dull folk. I put two shillings on the kitchen table and told her to lay an extra plate for dinner.

Her name doesn't matter, what matters is what she did to me and this was two-fold. There was something alluring to her in my profession as a boxer. In her mind there was a simple equation: strength, power and youth equalled virility. After the first few days I realised that her and her husband no longer slept in the same bed. After the first week she had lowered her neckline and fixed me with enough seductive glances to give me little doubt that she no longer wanted to sleep alone. Before my next bout with Peter Smith it had begun, and when it begins for a boxer the decision is irrevocable.

BOXING

PRESTON PUBLIC HALL,
Wednesday, April 1st, 1953

Doors open 6.45   Commence 7.30 prompt

Programme . . . . . . 3d.

All Seats Bookable at
THOS. HODGSON'S, 1a FLEET ST., PRESTON   Tel. 4723

Leyland Printing Co. Ltd.

Again I had to travel north, this time to Smith's home town, twelve days after we had met in Preston. The date still rings around my head: April 13th. I often wonder whether it was a psychological reaction rather than any real depletion of my physical ability to box, because boxers are always told that chastity is a pre-requisite to winning. I remember Bert used to put it most vividly, he would say "Boxers should only explode in one thing – and that's the ring!" Having been told this as though it were a cardinal tenet to success, when I did transgress, in my mind I had already lost. As we traced the same route to Huddersfield as to Preston, my psyche couldn't have been more contrasting than twelve days earlier. Come the fight I let Smith's style irritate me more than it normally would have. His square jabs and lilting backslides seemed effeminate and decentred my focus. Whether my body was truly wasted or whether I had riddled my brain and prematurely spent myself, by the time Smith had his inevitable eight rounds my strength had been dissolved.

Of course at the time I never owned up to my illicit philandering. Smith had won on a points decision and when people asked me about it I ran out a tale that the judges from Huddersfield were prejudicial towards their own. Boxing in his home town was the most fortunate coincidence of the night, as I could ward them off the scent of randy housewife, one I was sure clung to me wherever I went. I guess that was the introduction of shame. Although I lamented the loss of my beautiful consistency, I did so mainly in her arms. Some urges can divide the single-minded until they realise they must give way. If that is a failing then I failed, but I can't regret it. My unbeaten paradise went with a frustrated and buxom landlady who had fallen out of love and leaned temptingly over a kitchen table. And so we continued; in the kitchen, where it had all begun, in the front room, on the stairs, sometimes we even managed to make it to the comfort of a bed – mine or hers, it didn't matter. If only Jack Turner could have seen my secret, but I think he would have been more jealous than mad.

A week after, I was back in the ring and back at the Colston Hall. The irrecoverable loss of my precious record had been a disappointment, but I had to prove it was not going to turn into a malaise. I was fighting Jack Thornbury, who years later would become a chief magistrate in Bromley, Kent and send me a letter reminiscing.

I felt good as the bout began; I had him down briefly in the first round. As the fight progressed I had no reason to fear that I wasn't going to reinstate victory on my record. Then in the fifth everything unravelled. Thornbury hit me above the eye and I felt a thin line of pain sting sharply. In the tumult I had no time to give it any significance, but he kept going for the same spot. Again he connected. This time the hurt erupted massively and I fell on my knees. I felt the blood trickle down my forehead and I knew what had happened, but I got up quickly and we continued the confrontation. I knew I had to make it to the bell for respite, before he could hit the cut again. I had no idea how damaging it had been, it was my first professional wound. But Thornbury had a target, something definite to aim for, and boxers who have something to aim for are like little girls desperate for a doll; possessed with an illogical determination. And, just like a spoilt girl, he got what he wanted. For a third time Thornbury hit me above the eye, directly on the cut, and it blossomed open like a springtime flower. I was closer to the canvas than I had ever been before and I heard the referee shout one and then two. I hauled myself skyward, dazed but still determined. I could barely see the referee as he came between us and called for the fight to stop. There I stood, a warm mess, blinking through crimson darkness at my second defeat, as the adrenaline receded and paroxysms pulsed across my brow.

JAMES DEUCHERS
NOTED ALES

are available before and after the Fight at

THE PARK INN
(Opposite the Arena)

~~~~~~~~~~~~~~~~~~~~~~~~~~~~~~~

FRED SIMM,
B.B.B. of C. Promoter, Presents-

BOXING

AT THE

PARK LANE ARENA, SUNDERLAND,

ON

SATURDAY, 9th MAY, 1953.

Commencing at 3-15 p.m.

Programme 3d.

~~~~~~~~~~~~~~~~~~~~~~~~~~~~~~~

REMEMBER !
JAMES DEUCHERS PRODUCTS HAVE
THAT KNOCK=OUT EFFECT ! !

W H. FORSTER (Printers) Ltd., 22 Brougham Street, Sunderland.   Tel. 2324.

CHAPTER 11

JACK TURNER

The cut swelled over my eye for a day and then began to heal, but it was sore for a good while and liable to re-open if it was touched with any force. It is the kind of thing that is important to a boxer's business, something a manager should take into consideration when arranging a boxer's next fight. Not Jack Turner. But then boxers were never a long term investment to him, perhaps because with only one good eye he couldn't see that far. He told me there would be no postponement of my next fight which was scheduled two weeks after Thornbury. He wanted me back in the gym immediately.

I was to fight Eric Billington in Sunderland. We were the same age, but he had been fighting as a pro for six years and knew everything about the life. His precocity had given him a head start and his experience was much greater. Perhaps his experience would have prevented him climbing into bed with a woman directly after losing two bouts. Perhaps he deliberately wouldn't have passed on that advice if he had known what I was doing in the rooms of my boarding house.

When he has lost, a man will always look to numerous definitions as to why. Even if he is gracious and bows in acknowledgement to his superior, he cannot avoid ruminating on causes beyond his volition. It is not necessarily being a bad loser, because even the most out-boxed fighter can land a lucky punch and win. It is rather the realisation that any number of happenings, chance, fate or the machinations of a power beyond understanding, can set an irrecoverable course.

And so whilst it was true that I was still breaking that boxing commandment, it is also true that, in what he thought of as dedication, Jack accompanied me to Sunderland. The night before the fight, he got completely mined out of his skull on booze and proceeded to turn into a midnight bard, telling of his ballroom dancing class and the sexual endeavours he had wrangled from the women he danced with. The irony was unbearable, as was his monotonous voice that meandered about our room until all the energy from drinking had been expended and he fell unconscious. I woke at my usual early hour the next morning and by the time of the evening fight I started to feel the restless drowsiness of sleep deprivation. Jack, who was supposed to further my career, could have done no more to sabotage than hold my arms behind my back whilst my opponent set about my face. Billington won on points after eight. By the last couple of rounds I could barely move my feet, except to pivot as Billington orbited around me. That was three losses and it looked like a streak.

From the first moment I laid eyes on Jack Turner, bawling away like he had a demon inside him, I had a gut instinct not to get involved with him. He had been a boxer himself and by the account of those who had seen him, he was a tall jab-and-run fighter. In the late 1920s he had beaten Cast Iron Casey, who had been the northern area middle-weight champion after he beat Len Harvey's old bugbear Jock McAvoy. He then lost to Len himself when tilting at the Empire crown in the same division. But Jack's career had mainly been on the booths, he got nowhere near to being a contender. He was far more prominent as a manager and somehow managed to bring a lot of excellent fighters under his misguidance. While I was with him he had several excellent boxers such as Teddy Peckham, who was southern area feather-weight champion, who I always thought Jack had ruined, and Peter Fay and Gordon Goodman, bantam and lightweight contenders respectively. Notice how they were only contenders, because Jack would have them top of the bill one fight and next they would be opening up for someone with far less skill at some rotten hall where the promotion would have turned the Irish off potatoes. This was because Jack thought any money was good money. He cared less about the quality of the bout or the progress of the fighter than getting a cut of the proceeds. This was why I was back in the ring two weeks after a cut, or why casualties on the booths were always rushed out of sight and given a quick bucket of water over the head.

Jack's treatment of Peter Fay was the most outrageous. He arranged a bout in which he told Peter that he would be fighting a boxer a class below him, which meant Peter losing a few pounds in weight. This he did with considerable effort, devoted to his craft. Then, arriving at the venue on fight night, he found himself matched in his usual bantamweight division, his opponent several pounds heavier. Apparently Jack was apologetic but still enthusiastic that Peter could win, excusing himself by citing poor communication on the promoter's part. The reality turned out to be far more Machiavellian; Jack had a bet on Peter's opponent, the friend of a friend. Other than this being illegal, the moral revulsion everybody felt when they heard this bothered Jack far less than that Peter had actually won. And then there were Ted Mason and Dudley Cox, both boxers who had prospects that, under the tutelage of Jack Turner, dissolved into a resigned acceptance of stagnation. Mickey Duff, when he did have dealings with Jack, said he only did so because he had good fighters that he could get cheaply. Jack was like a train line that only went halfway to your destination; if you were to go any further you knew you'd have to get off and find alternative transport. And also there was the distraction of the fairground. If you boxed professionally for Jack then you performed on the booths too. The booths were wonderful, an absolute joy for a young man who could handle himself, or for mediocre pros who wanted the extra money. However, for a boxer with pretensions to titles and fame, or even of the artistry of his sport, it was like a young girl turning up at her wedding and finding an aspidistra as the floral bouquet.

Jack had been Freddie Mills' Promoter when his brother was Freddie's Manager in the late 1930s, although he told young boxers that he had been Mills' Manager. Unsurprisingly Mills had ceased his working relationship with both Turner brothers by the time he came in amongst the titles. Jack didn't even know a world champion when he had one. Mills would have probably stayed a contender, like Ted Mason and Dudley Cox, if he hadn't got away from Jack. At the nadir of my boxing career Jack Turner had nothing for me, no idea why I was losing and he was not someone I could trust to confide in. I'm sure he thought that I was one of his promising young boxers who was experiencing the inevitable, unavoidable failure, which to Jack was not even failure, because he couldn't imagine anything different. To him failure was natural, like the end of a flower's bloom. For failure there must first be some kind of expectation or hope, but in Jack there was neither of these and so he did nothing to try and halt my decline.

I continued travelling North, this time to Manchester for the completion of my trilogy against Peter Smith. It was one-a-piece after two – this was the decider. I went the inevitable eight rounds and lost a decision that wasn't even close. Afterwards, back on the South Coast, the Colonel attempted what Jack seemed completely oblivious to. He didn't get angry or sentimental, just said that something had to be done, to which I agreed. Then he paused and, as if it had occurred to him in that moment, he said, in his well-heeled voice with almost child-like astonishment at his own thought "I say Paul, you're not fucking are you?" There was no way I could deny it.

CHAPTER 12

DONKEY SEASON

The Colonel knew enough of love and desire to recognise that my affair with the landlady was a fleeting infatuation. He used a more lasting and platonic infatuation to suggest that I move in with him and Eric. The simplest solution, to remove me from her proximity and nullify the temptation, had meaning for my boxing career beyond the mere severance. Until now the Colonel had been only on the periphery of my life, coming to occasional bouts, taking me out afterwards, but having no real effect on my boxing. The first significant thing he did was to speak to Jack about how my fights were being organised. He ensured that Jack didn't arrange any more until he told him that I was ready. Jack's method would have been to keep plunging me into fights and wring me dry of whatever profit he could, until it became obvious that continuing would be an embarrassment and he could make nothing more. Thanks to the Colonel's intervention I had my longest stretch away from fighting since I had begun as a professional.

The irony was that having as much time as I needed away from boxing, the affair with my landlady would not have been a problem. But both the ending of my affair and time, were gifts from the strategic hand of one man. To disregard one because of the other would have been almost a violation of his patronage. If temptation remained at such close quarters it would have taken more will power than I could muster to break away. The second significant thing that the Colonel suggested, was that I move in with him and Eric. The best action was the swift one, I didn't want any emotional final meeting, tears, or explanation. I left when she was out and paid her husband my due rent.

Life with the Colonel provided many distractions to assuage the lack of intense training, with no imminent fights. For a start there was the novelty of living in a hotel. When the Colonel had said that I should move in with him, it wasn't his own property that he invited me to, but the Brookhurst Hotel in Highcliffe. He and Eric lived an itinerant life, their only responsibility was to themselves and they had the money and connections to please whatever whim took them. They would slip around the country, following the racing calendar, the shooting season, the Colonel's want of a particular single malt or the food at a favourite restaurant. They rarely planned any of these things. This kind of spontaneity was often too impetuous for packing and they left a complex trail of luggage behind them. It was nothing for the Colonel buy everything new at a local tailor. Sometimes the luggage would catch up with them and they would feign surprise, like an adult finally receiving the toys he had wished for as a child.

This was how the Colonel had lived all his life. In the military he had gone from wars to colonial postings to other wars and then bases around Britain. After the army he had been the Royal Equerry for a time, due to his skill with horses. He was a very modern aristocrat. Eric, meanwhile, had come to this style of life much later. As a newlywed he had been tempted by the wages the Colonel offered to abandon his wife and go on an extensive trip abroad. By the time they got back to England Eric's wife, in a pique of jealousy, had found someone else to love. And that was that. Without ties, Eric too became a wanderer. Because of my own troubles with a woman in 1955, I joined them.

Whilst we were living at Brookhurst the Colonel shot a donkey. The donkey lived in a field overlooked by the Colonel's bedroom window and had been braying every day for quite some time. The morning the incident happened we were eating breakfast in the Colonel's room. He summoned Eric to fetch his twelve-bore, which Eric did without question or change of expression. He handed the gun to the Colonel, who then asked him to open the window. The

Colonel pointed the gun, flexed his shoulders and arms slightly, looked down the barrel and fired. The explosion hurt my ears and the room smelled of cordite. When my ears stopped ringing, I could no longer hear the donkey's incessant noise. I went over to the window and looked out, and there it lay motionless on the grass. Distraught, I asked the Colonel why he had done it, protesting that the animal was innocent and more than likely an asset to its owner. "Quite right, Paul, but there was nothing else to be done. I have complained several times to the farmer." About an hour or so later a local Constable paid the Colonel a visit, saying that he had no other choice but to report the matter. Months later the Colonel received a telegram. He had been fined forty pounds for shooting the donkey out of season. He had not known that they were ever in season, the joke of which made it almost worth the forty pounds. The ease and assurance with which the Colonel did everything, whether it was entertaining the whole bar, hosting a party or shooting a donkey, seemed to communicate a greater knowledge of life, one that could take you anywhere. He was a mesmeriser and I was taken in.

PART THREE

TOP OF
THE BILL

ON THE TELEVISION
WESTERN AREA TITLE FIGHT
THE REST OF '54
THE NEW FOREST
LONDON'S BRUTAL GRAVITY
THERE'S NO BUSINESS LIKE SHOW BUSINESS
THOMAS À BECKET, LONDON 1955
THE ITALIAN JOB
THE CAFÉ ROYALE
A SAVAGE SYSTEM

CHAPTER 13

ON THE TELEVISION

The lights from the cameras turned the pavilion into a wet hot-house of baying fiends; hotter than it usually was in a boxing arena. Moisture drained from bodies and floated into the heavy, depressing air that was full of weighty, saturated gases. Dripping vapour oppressed the crowd, who shouted and panted, breathing in the salted firmament. A corona of light seemed to shine around the ring, under which the cameras filmed whatever desperate and eye-aching pugilism was fought out.

Back in the early fifties, because televised boxing was new, it wasn't as controlled an affair as it is now and was readily accepted in people's minds as entertainment. Soon, attention became more focused on an elite group of fighters in order to make more money, but back in the early fifties the logic was less cynical. They knew that any fight could be a good fight and any fight could be a bad fight whatever the hype, and they didn't pick contests purely on their proximity to the most prestigious titles. I think that there was something of convenience and cost about it as well. When cameras and sound equipment were heavy and industrial they were expensive to transport and set up. So it happened that in the run up to my fight with Rees Moore, with a single victory behind me to obscure the memory of four losses, Jack told me to tell everyone that I was going to be on television. Of course, Jack was more excited than anyone else, thinking, as he always did, of cheques with longer numbers scrawled across them.

There weren't any fighters who were anything other than locally famous on the bill that night. In fact, the majority were from some corner of the West Country, the event being held at the Winter

Director of Entertainments :
I. DAVIES

Pavilion Manager :
D. S. ASHMAN

Winter Gardens Pavilion

Weston-super-Mare

Grand Boxing

Programme

TELEVISED 9.35 to 10.20 p.m.

Promoted by the

WESTON-SUPER-MARE SPORTSMEN'S ORGANISATION (B.B.B. of C.)

President—*His Worship The Mayor*, Ald. D. H. MILLER-BARSTOW, M.A., J.P.

Chairman—J. TRAPNELL, Esq.
Vice-Chairman—Councillor Mrs. M. E. Lucas
Chairman Matchmaking Committee—C. PERKINS, Esq.
Chairman Charities Committee— C. P. OXLEY, Esq.
Chairman Publicity Committee—R. L. HARRISON, Esq.
Hon. Medical Officer— DR. RICHARD ALFORD

———◆———

MONDAY, 21st SEPTEMBER, 1953
at 8.0 p.m.

———◆———

Hon. Organising Secretary and Treasurer	-	MR. N. W. J. WEYMOUTH
Hon. Assistant Secretary	-	Miss N. A. YATES
Hon. Auditor	-	MR. C. MAXWELL
Hon. Chief Steward	-	Mr. P. HENLEY

Programme 6d.

Gardens in Weston-super-Mare. It was how things were run. Many boxers didn't have the prospects to merit the outlay on a trip across the provinces. So it was mainly West Country boxers on the bill, each with their own pinhead of support, gathered from amongst local boxing aficionados. And they were going to be on the television! Unfortunately we found out that the television signal, beamed up to London and from there out to the rest of the country, could only transmit as far West as Exeter. Torquay is located several miles further South West. However, plenty of my fans were in Weston-super-Mare that night to witness events firsthand. Others too crossed the imaginary borderline demarcating the inclusion of Exeter and the exclusion of Torquay to find a set that was within range.

That September night I was to fight Rees Moore, who would become the welterweight champion of Wales. He was a fast, strong hitter who loved to box on the retreat like a tank in reverse still firing shells at the enemy. From within the shining television camera corona I could barely see anything beyond the ropes. But I could hear enough and smell enough to be able to know what was going on beyond the lights. Of course, there was a commentator too, which was new. He sat at a desk immediately below the ring, behind his microphone. Between each round I could hear his voice, its crystal clear pitch vibrating amongst the din. All my senses were coordinated for extreme concentration. Losing Rees Moore for a few seconds, my ears unwaveringly switched to the BBC man as he solely shouldered the burden of relaying the action to the people watching at home.

Perhaps Moore found himself intimidated by the lights, because he fought like a businessman pays tax. True to his reputation, he spent most of the eight rounds stepping back. I was ahead on points by the seventh and in that round I came close to stopping his incessant backpedalling. It was only his expertise in the craft that saved him. In the final round the crowd whipped themselves up into excitement, sensing a knockdown as I threw myself at his diminishing figure. It was undisciplined and petulant. Moore retaliated by cutting me along my eyebrow. However, the fight was already decided before I introduced some drama at the end. Despite the hot pulse of the television cameras it was a somewhat spiritless event.

In purely boxing terms appearing on the television was like a parent's praise and no one who really mattered thought anything of it. When people came up to me and, with enthusiastic exaggeration, said they'd heard that I was on the television and that I must be a big star, I always just smiled. There were other, much more heeded sources for the appraisal of a boxer: the liquor-lit conversations of a tree-topping coterie, the printed assessment of respected boxing writers, the mob's excitement. The convenience and naivety with which television operated made it's validation unimportant, but it wouldn't be long until television and money always appeared inseparable in a promoter's mind. The broadcast from Weston-super-Mare was birdsong before the dawn.

It was the restoration of my breakout flourish of wins that got me my first steps in a London ring; a place on a big charity bill at Wembley town hall, promoted by Eddie Derfield. I was to fight Johnny Fish from Harlow, who was a big favourite with the Wembley crowd. He had just been nominated for an area title shot, yet after our fight, apart from a subsequent string of victories, his impressive career declined and he withered without glory. Fish certainly had a good chin. I won but was exasperated by a huge, looping right that failed to knock him down. In all my fight history, I can recall only a few punches that come near to matching it. For this reason it dominates my memory of the fight, to the extent where I can remember little else. Afterwards I was consumed with disbelief that I had not knocked him down, which is the most secret pleasure of winning: dissatisfaction despite success. Something you can never empathise with, when losing. But I had been scared by Fish not going down, like a general who

BOXING

WATFORD TOWN HALL

BROADCAST NIGHT

TUESDAY, NOV. 24th, at 8 p.m.

PROMOTER: MR. A. E. MALLETT, B.B.B.C.

EIGHT (3 min) ROUNDS WELTERWEIGHT CONTEST

ALF DANAHAR v. PAUL KING

Bethnal Green. Southern Area Welterweight Champion. Sensational contest with Champion, Wally Thom.

Torquay. Defeated Rees Moore in Televised contest Sept 21st. Also beaten Eric Billington, Peter Smith, Eric Skidmore, Noel Sinfield.

THIS CONTEST WILL BE BROADCAST at 8.30 p.m.

Six (2 min) Rounds Bantamweight Contest

JIM FREW v. MICHAEL LUCY

Watford

Shepherds Bush

Six (2 min) Rounds Light Heavyweight Contest

SID CAIN v. JOHNNY HALL

Watford. Your popular local boxer.

Dunstable. Defeated Terry Donovan at last show.

Eight (3 min) Rounds Lightweight Contest

ROY COLES v. KEVIN DUFFY

Weston-Super-Mare. Beaten Laurie Henry, Joe Lloyd, Len Grainger, Freddy Leek.

Hillingdon. Undefeated at Watford. Beaten Cyril Evans, Maurice Murfitt, etc.

EIGHT (3 min) ROUNDS WELTERWEIGHT CONTEST

LEO MALONEY v. GORDON KEARNS

Hillingdon. Defeated Fred Morris, Ron Ball, Arthur Garrett, Johnny Pipe, Pat Gutteridge, Holt, Eddie King, Derek Cooke.

Shepherds Bush. 1953 I.S.B.A. Champion. Has beaten Johnny Maloney, the 1952 A.B.A. Champion. First appearance at Watford.

ALEX BUXTON, Light Heavyweight Champion of Gt. Britain, wearing his Championship Belt will be welcomed in the ring by his Worshipful The Mayor of Watford (Alderman A. G. Dillingham, J.P., C.C.)

Ringside 17/6 & 22/6 Grd. Floor 5/- 7/6 12/6 Stage 7/6 Balcony 5/- 7/6 & 12/6

TICKETS from Promoter A. E. Mallett, 27 Monmouth Rd., Watford (Watford 5120); Messrs. Elliotts, 14 High St., Watford (Watford 4238); Mr. A. D. Fountain, 864 Kenton Lane, Harrow Weald (Grimsdyke 197); A. Grimsdell, 158 High, Watford; The Manor Travel Agency, 23 Victoria Road, Ruislip (Ruislip 6511); Breans Coaches, 74 Bury Road, Hemel Hempstead (Boxmoor 640)

LICENSED BAR

fires his gun with the longest range and watches it fall short of the enemy.

Afterwards came the televised sequel to the Moore fight. This time it was in Watford against Alf Danahar. He had won the Southern Area welterweight title in 1949, defended it successfully until 1952 and because it was not resurrected until 1958, effectively remained champion beyond even his retirement. This was 1953 and around the turn of the decade he was ranked sometime second and sometime third best welterweight in the country. He was a boxer with pedigree. However, after losing to the eventual champion, Wally Thom, in an eliminator for the British crown, he had won four lonely fights amidst a swell of losses.

For much of the build-up to the fight I was experiencing the growth of public praise; Bournemouth boxing fans were beginning to adopt me and mentions in the national press were becoming as frequent as in the Torquay weeklys. I remember the Colonel becoming excited one morning as he read through his copy of *The Times* in which they had devoted a line of print to the forthcoming bout. Added to this it was to be my second appearance on television and boxing fans from around the country who owned a TV set, were about to be reintroduced to my righteous style of boxing.

The classic early BBC commentary team of Raymond Glendenning and W. Barrington Dalby were behind the desk at ringside. Before the fight there was a presentation, the local Mayor fulfilling his civic duty by presenting Alex Burton, then the light-heavyweight champion of Britain, with a certificate of merit won against Dennis Powell. In the dusty corridor I could hear this lionisation of the victor for the television cameras. It felt like the domestication of an animal instinct.

It was this feeling that I experienced at the end of the fight, with the television cameras catching the mêlée as both camps rushed into the ring and I was grabbed and shaken and buffeted. I felt the warm afterglow of victory shining on me the next morning, sitting in front of a selection of newspapers proclaiming my victory, 'King too smart for Danahar', 'King Scores at Watford', 'Danahar Beaten by Young Welter', 'Torquay Welterweight's Triumph', 'Danahar Beaten'. Reading of your own triumph across the back-pages of the newspapers for the first time: it is the best cure for a hangover I have ever found.

The fight itself provided much more entertainment for the viewers than the previous time. It helped that I had faced a fighter who had none of the reticence of Rees Moore. Len had wanted me to box Danahar. In the first rounds Danahar stole my style, which was probably his too, but it felt like I was being invaded. I had to retaliate by being that self more than he was. The fight bloomed. In the fourth I hit Danahar with a combination that staggered him viciously. In the sixth my youthfulness almost ended him.Danahar was old but his time-tested ways managed to save him. In the seventh, from necessity, he flashed both fists at me, striving for the opening, but he didn't have the stamina and I put him, winded, in a neutral corner, desperately trying to inflate his lungs. He valiantly stayed up for the whole of the final three minutes, his strength of will held his body stable as I breached his enervated defence again and again. When the bell sounded, the decision was unanimous.

The next day, in the shadow of the headlines, I read the reporters' quotes of Barrington Dalby's commentary 'King is decidedly promising' and 'quite first-rate'. It was high praise indeed from one with such authority. The night before, with bottles of whisky and gin empty behind the bar, the public rooms of East Sheen were said to have echoed with a prophetic cry. Len Harvey's glass extended towards me and those assembled heard it "There stands the next welterweight champion of Great Britain!"

Trades Club Reception, 1954

CHAPTER 14

WESTERN AREA TITLE FIGHT

With public success comes public expectation. I caught the train down from Paddington; a Torquay newspaper had sent one of their men to meet me at the station. I was ushered into the back seat of a taxi, the reporter smiling over at me, in his hands a shorthand notepad and a pen. It was a week before Christmas, 1953. This was no usual interview. The reporter said that they had thought it might be an idea to take me back to my old school, just to say a few words of encouragement to the children, a sort of 'look what you can achieve' festive message. It would make a great story too, he said.

I found myself herded on to the stage at Audley Park Christmas assembly, in the same sports hall where I had first thrown a gloved punch. The headmaster introduced me to the youthful faces staring up in silence and asked me to say those few words of encouragement. This was the bad, nervous type of adrenaline. Adrenaline in a boxing ring is good. You need it. For improvised public speaking it is only a hindrance. So I spluttered a few words, what they were I mercifully don't remember. The stress of the situation has wiped my mind clean. No doubt the journalist recorded them in his article, but if I ever read it, I certainly didn't keep it. I would rather be in the ring with the Boston Tar Baby than on that stage again.

The hot light of the public gaze when it was lauding my boxing, was a thrill. When its glare made inescapable what was demanded of a public figure, it was uncomfortable. Somewhat more relaxing, but still a duty, was the special reception the local Trades Club laid on, with myself as guest of honour. It was all pleasantries and congratulations and thanks for their support. Afterwards it was a relief to stop being Torquay's son, Civic Hero, and just be my natural self and out for a drink amongst people I knew.

In Torquay I managed a few weeks of liberty from professional demands. I drank plenty, ate too much, met girls and then slouched back to Bournemouth and the dull discipline of training. Soon after getting back, coming in to the gym one morning, Jack approached me with his one good eye shining and a smile underneath it. He told me he'd done it, he'd got me a big one, a shot for the Western Area welterweight title against Terry Ratcliffe.

I was ecstatic at the prospect. All the glory and praise built up from winning, all the disillusion of losing, the moments when you doubt if it was ever a good idea to get into boxing in the first place, this was all now outshone by the prospect of a title shot. I remember the feeling of absolute certainty and unquestionable vindication. I doubted very much however, Jack's claim that he had engineered it. There is absolutely no way he spent his Christmas lobbying for my progression; he probably just answered the phone. The powers that be had recognised, from what they had seen and heard of me in the ring, that I was a rightful contender. It was my work, not his, that had me on the canvas for a belt. But, charlatan that he was, he tried to claim credit anyway.

At the end of my trip home to Torquay a carbuncle had grown on my arm like a hideous overnight flower. After much pain it cleared. But then, with the day of my first title looming, a foul garden of boils began to sprout on my back. Medical expertise was quickly sought and the doctor confirmed with formal recognition what we already knew, that the fight was off.

However, the purse and puppet-string pullers didn't quite see it that way, you might even say that they were glad of my pulling out. They had the lure of a title fight and all the money that meant, but no fit contender. Knowing that a rematch would be arranged soon enough and the punters would eventually get their entertainment, they saw no reason to pass up on the swell they had already created. I would have to be seen to pull out at a moment so late that postponement and refunds would have been impractical. To verify this fiction they drew in their long arm and took me up to Bristol, so that I would be there for the announcement of the abandonment of the title bout. Then they would usher me into the shadows and pull in a replacement fighter. I felt sympathy for my own fans, but my business was boxing and had I not complied, my re-match would have vanished. I imagined the collective groan from the fans as they turned up at Colston Hall in freezing January only to see Bobby Johnson's name pasted over mine and 'Title' blanked out on the posters.

So I watched, itching and frustrated, as my mate Bobby Johnson sent Ratcliffe scattering to the deck in the first round for a count of six and then spiritedly lost his way to an obviously superior pugilist. The new date was rearranged almost immediately for February 22nd. Having already trained to near peak condition, I was left with over a month of no purpose and a mind that wanted to revolt against all this. It was not what I was used to; a string of fights where training was disrupted by the real thing and periods of no training, or little, when I could indulge myself in prohibited behaviour. The perpetual concentration of almost two months daily training was a true test of my will to box.

During this time, people talked amongst themselves of my fight and they began to coax out excitement and speculation. Somebody (from the *Daily Mirror*) spoke to me and then somebody else, or perhaps the same person realised, that my connection with Len and his pedigree was an easy headline. I guess journalists often have to make stories out of nothing and trust that almost anything can be interesting. When I mentioned that I sometimes telephoned Len Harvey, they had their narrative point number one. When I said I had bought a window-cleaning round to make

PAUL KING
WINDOW CLEANER

MODERATE
CHARGES
*
EFFICIENT
SERVICE
FULLY
INSURED
*
544 ASHLEY ROAD
PARKSTONE

WHO SAID BIGHEAD ?

CLEANING WINDOWS

I understand that Paul King the Torquay welter, is now living in Bournemouth and runs a window cleaning business with young Eddie Baker, the 17-year-old local lightweight. No doubt with his longer reach Paul does the top windows and leaves those on the ground floor to Eddie.

Paul King gets his boxing lessons by 'phone

Two telephone calls a week to a London pub are helping Paul King, 22 window-cleaner, toward a fight for the British welterweight title.

The man he rings is Len Harvey, former holder of three British titles, who now keeps a London pub. He reports his training progress to Harvey, and asks for advice on any points of ringcraft which trouble him.

PERSONAL INTEREST

"I was asked to take an interest in the lad by a personal friend of mine, Colonel Forsyth, a real old sporting gentleman who lives in the same town as King - Torquay - and has taken a great interest in his career. It's a pleasure to do so. The lad is terribly keen and willing to learn, and I think he will lift the welterweight title if he isn't rushed". Harvey said.

some immediate cash, they had their narrative point number two. It was the most bizarre article that I can recall from all my time boxing. First they strung out my mention of telephoning Len into my being trained from London by two phone calls a week, then they made me take my ladder and bucket out to the front of my house and pose a few rungs up. They even prompted Len to comment on my window-cleaning, 'You can't do a heavy job and be a boxer,' he reportedly said. This was the pre-fight frenzy offered up to the *Mirror* reading public.

Other papers were more concerned with boxing and one featured Freddie Mills giving his opinion on myself and Ratcliffe. He spoke of how Ratcliffe hadn't lived up to his promise in 1953, of how he had been expected to rise amongst the top of the British welter-weights but hadn't quite made it. Of me he didn't have much to say, but that 1953 had been good for me and the fans should be excited that it wasn't going to be easy for Ratcliffe. Nevertheless, he seemed to say that it was inevitable that Ratcliffe would win.

Ratcliffe's back story was indeed impressive. He had topped the amateur game at welterweight and in 1950 he had been British amateur champion and also champion at the Empire Games. Then he had started a professional career and won seventeen straight fights. He was with Jack Solomons, boxing all the promotions at the White City and Earls Court. But he certainly wasn't unbeatable. The disappointing year that Freddie Mills had alluded to, was largely down to a trio of bouts with the formidable Lew Lazar. Lazar had won all but two of his first thirty-six bouts, including ending the short career of Charlie Kray (brother to the twins), before succumbing to Wally Thoms in a British title fight. One of these fights was a draw, one was a loss. It was Ratcliffe who had given him that loss, beating him on points in their first encounter. Then Lazar came back from defeat and knocked out Ratcliffe twice, one bout being an eliminator for the title shot that he would eventually lose to Thoms. Because boxing is all about the story, fighting one man three times in a year is always blown up into a rivalry whether it is true or fictitious. I experienced it myself in the early days with Pring. The drama leads to extra pressure and coming out of it like Ratcliffe can affect a boxer, or so I hoped.

The Western Area title had become like crown jewels after a revolution; the belt still glittered but no one had worn it for twenty-three years. Just why this discontinuity had occurred I don't know. When it had last been fought for in 1931, it had been called the West of England welterweight title. The two old fighters who had boxed that year were George Rose and Dixie Brown. Both still resided in Bristol and both were invited as honorary guests at this resurrection. Dixie Brown, even though he lost that night, holds a special place in Bristolian boxing folklore. He was a black St Lucian who had emigrated to Wales after the Great War, before moving to Bristol. Soon he became a booth boy. This was when it was bare-knuckled fighting. After turning professional and coming in for all kinds of prejudices, he had fought George Rose. Such was the local love for Dixie that when a couple of years later he lost his sight after a brutal fight, enough money was donated to afford the devout Catholic a trip to Lourdes in the hope of a miracle. Unfortunately Dixie was never beatified and is still best remembered as a black boxer in a white world. Though he couldn't see us perform, he must have loved the smells and the noises of the ring.

I shook his hand that night, and it was in consolation that he shook mine, because this wouldn't be the story of a beltless boxer if I had won. How I failed that night; it is painful to look back on. Not because I was humiliated, but because after seven rounds I had the fight and then by twelve it was no longer mine. In only the third Ratcliffe was down for an eight count and by the seventh I could see him splayed on the canvas unconscious. That was the error, the uncorrected error of my career. When I should have boxed him, I tried to kill him. All the pleas of Len Harvey couldn't stop me. All the hindsight in the world wouldn't have stopped me.

COLSTON HALL
BRISTOL
Promoter and Matchmaker : TOM PYPER
Monday, Jan. 11th at 7-30 p.m.
BOXING
Licensed by the B.B.B. of C. (1929)
Welterweight Championship
OF THE WEST OF ENGLAND
12 (3-min.) Rounds at 10st. 7lbs.
TERRY — PAUL
RATCLIFFE v. KING
(Bristol) — (Torquay)

Heavyweight Contest, Six (3- min.) Rounds
Cliff PURNELL (Bath) **v. Deny POWELL** (London)

Sensational Welterweight Contest, Six (3-min.) Rds.
Bobby JOHNSON v. Derek COOKE
Plymouth) — (London)

Lightweight Contest, Six (3-min.) Rounds
Tommy RYAN v. Mike HUGHES
(London) — (Netherhaven)

Welterweight Contest, Six (3-min.) Rounds
Johnny WILLIAMSON v. Freddy SMITH
(Gloucester) — (Weston)

Elimination Contest for the Lightweight
Championship of the West of England.
Ten (3-min.) Rounds at 9st. 9lbs.
ROY — HARRY
Coles v. Legge
(Weston) — (Poole)
OTHER CONTESTS
TIME PERMITTING

TICKETS 3/6, 5/-, 7/6, 10/6, 15/-, 21/-
RINGSIDE 21/- and 30/-

From Colston Hall, Tel. 21768, 10 a.m.—6 p.m.;
Sats. 10 a.m.—2 p.m.; also Milton's Library,
Fishponds; Co-op. Stores, Castle St.; C.W.S.,
Broad Quay; Harris, Sports Depot, St. Stephen's
Street.

WILLSONS, PRINTERS, LEICESTER

In the ring I was in a different world and by the eleventh, when it was no longer superiority that drove me to a knock-out, but a despairing necessity, I was where Ratcliffe had been in the third. The last round, I try to forget.

The Colonel and Eric were there but there was no consolation party afterwards. There was just Len, with his great heart full of compassion and empathy. All the long night he quietly bathed my eyes and bruises with a hot towel so that I wouldn't have to face tomorrow with two black eyes, saving me from the reminder of my wounds, soothing my disappointment, salving my ego.

CHAPTER 15

THE REST OF '54

Life after boxing occasionally brought with it whispers and rumours. There was no mass fraternity back in the 1950s, but everybody was at least familiar with anyone they didn't know personally. This was enough to raise interest, whether we were laughing at someone's misfortune or cursing their good luck. Tales would circulate round the old boys, who had dispersed but were still connected through someone or other. One such tale was the story of Pat Gutteridge's honour, so much more exciting and noteworthy than that of the average ex-fighter. I heard it from different people each time, acted out in instalments and lasting a quarter of a pint in telling.

In brief it went like this: being an East End lad participating in a sport with such connections to the underworld, he was bound to come across men that would offer him a way of earning money much greater than he could earn through any legitimate business. Being of the same generation as the twins whose notoriety went nationwide, the chance that he would have come across them in either amicability or hostility was a good one. As it happens, or so the story was told, the Krays were disposed to make of Gutteridge an employee and an ally. This was the original instalment. Years later I heard a follow-up over half a pint.

Having carried out whatever deeds ex-boxers do when acting under the patronage of a criminal organisation, Gutteridge had landed himself a three year prison sentence. At the conclusion of his incarceration, as he walked out of the gates, a prison guard handed him a set of keys and pointed to a brand new Volvo (I heard it told as a Rover too), which apparently was exactly what

Gutteridge expected. What else he thought his due I don't know, but on opening the glove compartment of the vehicle he found several tight wads of fresh notes. The amount is another matter of debate. One person said quite authoritatively that he had been bought a pint that very night out of those fresh notes and Gutteridge had said his earnings (for he considered them earnings), were three thousand pounds. Others I have talked to assumed, when hearing this figure, that Pat didn't actually want to divulge the extent of the gratitude that had been maturing over three slow years, but that the actual amount reached five thousand pounds or thereabouts. However, these were moot points because the one thing they all agreed on, which seemed to be the moral of Gutteridge's story, was what he was in prison for. In every instance it's stated that when asked he replied "For keeping my mouth shut." Everyone would then fall silent, as though mulling over this mysterious pronouncement. Then somebody would always say "Now that's what I call a hard man."

This is not an idle anecdote, I am telling it for a reason. My next fight, after the disappointment of losing the Western Area belt, was against Pat Gutteridge at Wembley Town Hall. As a London boy, Gutteridge would have the crowd, that much I knew. As you might be able to guess from the tales of his post-boxing life, his style in the ring was never the most subtle. He employed constant intimidation and it was put to good use. Skilful boxers do not command fear until they are observed in action. Gutteridge didn't need to do anything, he was menacing as an ordinary man. Beyond the ropes he was like an ancient harvestman, he had two scythes for arms that swept in huge hooking arcs. All his hits were contained in these shots. He liked to push the fight, as I did, and although he exuded menace, I am sure that there was some fear in the self-knowledge that he was limited in what he could do.

And so it happened as the opening bell rang. It was frenetic and desperate from the start, the sense of an ending never too far away. But it was also unexpected when it came; in the second

WEMBLEY TOWN HALL

CHARITY BOXING TOURNAMENT

Licensed by B. B. B. of C.

Matchmaker : ***EDDIE DERFIELD***

TUESDAY, 4th MAY, 1954

at 8 p.m.

IN AID OF THE

EDGWARE & DISTRICT REFORM S.R.F.

round I was suddenly aware that I was looking at the lights above the ring. It must have come from my periphery, such a big hook that it travelled so far wide that I couldn't see it. Lying on my back I had to assume that's what put me there. I took most of the count to regain myself and fight the round out.

I cannot recall whether what happened next was intuition or design, but looking back after the fight it seemed the most obvious thing I could do. Here was someone who was better at my style than I was myself, and so I had to diversify and it worked. Afterwards Len called it boxing, as if I had been doing something different until now. I had waited for Gutteridge to unlock himself instead of trying to knock the door down. Because Gutteridge only had one speed, there wasn't much patience required, with a more reticent boxer I wouldn't have been able to do it. The fight wasn't totally clean; after a while he had realised that it wouldn't be to his advantage to keep it that way. There was plenty of in-fighting and holding and with his strength it was difficult to get away. Come the seventh Gutteridge couldn't keep the ferocity up anymore and a well-timed left and then a right stopped him for a nine count. He was sluggish and easily picked off after that, and I had him down again before the round was out. Then the count ran down and my fist and his body were hoisted up. The crowd had loved it, as had the press. 'Excitement for all, much of it provided by Paul King and Pat Gutteridge' read the *Weekly Sporting Review*.

So when I returned to Wembley Town Hall a few weeks later to fight Leo Maloney, I expected some enthusiasm to have lingered amongst the cognoscenti. Len had told me that he'd watched Maloney before and that I shouldn't expect him to simply wilt and not to spit. He was even more enthusiastic than usual about having me 'box' my opponent after the Gutteridge fight. I didn't care, I went out to end it quickly. I crowded Maloney with close flurries and didn't let him have a moment, not a single opportunity.

I must have hit plum on his weakness because after fifty seconds he'd been counted out.

By the summer the disappointment of the Ratcliffe fight was receding, especially as I had subsequently managed two knockouts. My next fight was to take place in Jersey, a fourth with that frustrating Yorkshire man, Peter Smith, who had tormented me when I had faltered and favoured bouts of amorousness over boxing. Unfortunately, my chance to even-out our record was spoilt when he pulled out and instead I was to be meeting Pat Gutteridge again, who held little fear for me after my mastery of him in Wembley. I felt put out that all my training would be wasted on someone who was no progression for me. Of course, it was money and so far as I regarded boxing as 'simply a job' it was fine, but I wasn't being tested and without that, a job is all it was. Feeling despondent, in the few days I was in Jersey four pounds slipped into my waistband; the result of an over-zealous desire for chips. Weighing in at ten stone eleven pounds, the promoter Eddie Derfield refused point blank to let me box, which if this were 'just a job', would have meant a significant loss of earnings. So I doubled up my clothes when training and by the time of the weigh-in I had sweated it all out. Under the warm summer sky of the open-air stadium in St Helier, I put Gutteridge down twice and took him on points, untroubled and deliberate.

Facing George Happe in my next fight, my fortunes seemed to be growing. Happe was the second contender for the welterweight crown in 1954; at the time of our fight he was waiting for a re-match with Wally Thoms or a crack at Lew Lazar. That particular period was an excellent time for the British welterweight division. I was ranked seventh. There was Peter Waterman too, striving for greater altitude. It was all very tight. No one in the top ten was a forgone conclusion for anyone else. Suitably enough Terry Waltham, secretary of the British Boxing Board, was at ringside looking over our chances with an eye on the

☞ **PLEASE ORDER TICKETS AS EARLY AS
POSSIBLE TO AVOID DISAPPOINTMENT** ◀

BOXING Matchmaker: EDDIE DERFIELD BOXING

WEMBLEY TOWN HALL

3 min from Wembley Park Station   Buses 83, 16, 46 pass the door

TUESDAY 15th. JUNE   Doors open 6.30 p.m. Commence 8.0 p.m.

GRAND CHARITY BOXING TOURNAMENT IN AID OF EDGWARE AND DISTRICT S.R.F.

Important 8 (3 min) Rounds Welter-weight Contest at 10-9

PAUL KING

Torquay. *A new Welter sensation whom you asked to see after his grand winning contest with Pat Guttridge, also defeated Johnny Fish here.*

LEO MALONEY

Hillingdon. *A clever and classy box fighter, a great favourite with Wembley patrons. Remember his great contest here against Pat Guttridge and his terrific winning contest against highly rated Jack Thornbury.*

Grand 6 (3 min) Rounds Cruiser-weight Contest at 12-9

TONY DOVE v DON STOKER

Battersea. Former A.B.A. star   Torquay. Strong up & coming fighter

Attractive 6 (3 min) Rounds Welter-weight Contest at 10-2

KEVIN DUFFY v FRANK O'BRIEN

Hillingdon. Won his last 7 contests   Ireland. A strong two fisted fighter

6 (2 min) Rounds Light-weight Contest

BILLY KIERNAN v KEN LEWIS
Shepherds Bush   Jamaica

6 (2 min) Rounds Middle-wt Contest

RON POPELY v FRED BALIO
Rotherhithe   West Africa

Special 8 (3 min) Rounds Welter-weight Contest at 10-7

CHARLIE PAGE v DANNY GILL

Bethnal Green. Winning all along the   Bethnal Green. All action fighter
line. Defeated Gordon Kearns, etc.   defeated Ken Bebbington, etc.

21/- 15/- 10/6 7/6 5/- 3/6   Special Ringside 42/-

Ringside   Res   Res   Res   Unres

eliminators. 'Thom, Lazar or bust next time' was how the press analysed the stakes, and they applied it to both of us. Of course, I had to win first to get that option.

Edgware Town FC it was; boxing on the pitch in a summer of roofless rings. But George Happe almost murdered me in the first round. My confidence that I was stronger than him was a mistake. Not that he simply over-powered me, he did much more than that. As I thundered at him, his adept timing slipped my punches. Not in a completely defensive way; he was registering as many clean connections as I was air-shots. A stiff jab stunned me, an enthusiastic right stung my ear and a follow up with a merciless left had me draped over the bottom rope. Happe was now fired up, and I cowered and skulked for the rest of the round trying to avoid him. It was not a comfortable place for me and little good it did. I helped myself to a nine-second reprieve before the bell.

It was the worst first round I had boxed in my entire career, perhaps ever. Consequently, I am pleased to say that I lasted a full eight rounds, but not much else went right. I found him almost impossible to catch. I was forced to learn quickly and stop trying to avoid him. In that way I could at least absorb most of his punches with my forearms. After five more rounds of him slowly increasing his points score, he again knocked me down in the sixth and the seventh, both for a full nine. In the final round, as I was falling between 'the saddle and the ground', I had the Catholic notion that I could rescue the fight and knock him out with a single lucky or skilful punch. I attacked him, but it didn't work and I was left with the feeling that half my face was hanging off, flayed from my skull. Brutally seen to, I had faltered again in a consequential fight. A real contender to face, a test, a mark of actual progress and I had been brutally seen to.

Len had been ill in hospital around that time and had missed my humiliation. I am sure he would have been impressed with Happe's craft and no doubt disappointed with me. But he was back for my next fight against Jackie Braddock. I won against Braddock and I won with plenty of technique. Len, classic stylist as he was during his youth, could never agree with the way I boxed. He hadn't realised that for me it wasn't a choice; it was a necessity in order to overcome a natural aversion to pain. If I constantly attacked there was a certain amount of mayhem involved and I had a feeling of liberty. This is the best way I can describe it and yet there is more to it than that. For example, if you asked a smaller man to be a slugger, he would be incapable of sustaining big punches even if he managed to give the illusion for a while. Eventually he would lose assuredness and control, both essential elements in the battle of concentration and will that accompany physicality. When I boxed there was often an element of my own fear, which I would feed off and couldn't dismiss. I had to work with it and couldn't reconcile a more reserved approach. It was unlucky that Len had missed my destruction by a fighter with superior technique and witnessed my out-boxing of a fighter I found I could out-box. And so his futile attempts to disregard my natural propensity continued.

The Braddock fight was broadcast on television, straight after 'About Britain: A Journey with Richard Dimbleby to the Isle of Skye'. I still have the cutting from *The Radio Times*. It took place at Watford Town Hall, a major venue for London boxing at the time. At the time of our fight Braddock was still the Central Area champion and his brother was formerly the light-heavyweight champion of Britain, Frankie Johnson. He had boxing in his blood. Apparently Braddock was adept at embittering pretty young girls too. In the dressing room before the fight I was visited by the daughter of promoter Eddie Mallett and without explanation, requested by her to knock Braddock out. If I had been a different boxer she would have got her wish. As it was I was ruled by impetuous desire rather than cold thought. When Braddock took a six count I realised glory too soon, overstretched myself, and had to endure a full-length fight because of it. I had too many points for Braddock to ever successfully come back but he forced me into employing all my guile for the last four rounds, and that delighted Len. The hotel bar and then breakfast at Simpsons on The Strand followed, all under the direction of the Colonel, who was at the height of his charismatic luminosity. All the whiskey he drank couldn't make him seem intoxicated. People gathered round the bar to watch him perform as they had done round the ring for me hours earlier. I just sat and supped my light ales.

1954 ended with a fight on my home ground. It was to be an official civic appreciation of all the publicity that my boxing had brought to Torquay. The letter from the Corporation's Publicity Committee, signed by T. Elved-Williams, Town Clerk, had pleased me beyond words. I said 'home' but what I meant was: at least close enough to home for it to be regarded as a homecoming. Paignton shares Torbay with Torquay. I was in the ring with Rees Moore again, now Welsh welterweight champion. The fight held no of fear for me; I had already mastered him. His ultra-conservative style neutered any atmosphere that there was in the temporary marquee erected for the bout. He dropped away from me whenever he could and I chased, throwing enough points to have won by a large margin. The crowd managed to corral some enthusiasm in the final round when it was obvious that I would win. This engendered absolutely no passion from the Welsh champion, no desperate knock-out attempt, no desire to upset these people baying for his blood, just stoically backwards he went. At the end of the fight, even though not much had been achieved, we celebrated, and I sloped back to wherever I could find a bed.

If that was a tainted and ultimately worthless victory, then my next fight was simply forgettable. Roy Baird was another Celtic champion, or was about to be one a month after he beat me. The Northern Irishman ranked fourth contender for the British welterweight crown and this was another opportunity to prove myself against a boxer who mattered. The fight took place at Great Yarmouth's Hippodrome on the Norfolk Coast and my predominant memory is of Len's encouragement, 'Be first Paul, be first'. But it was useless. As had previously occurred in Jersey, I weighed in overweight. Again, confident I could lose the necessary weight without feeling too weak, I opted not to pay the five-pound fine. It was a bad decision and my weakness cost me.

However, after the fight, two good decisions were made. One: Len and the Colonel would decide when I was ready to fight again, which wasn't to be for three months. Two: that the Colonel and Eric would take an active interest in my fitness. The candle of hope flickered on for one more winter at least.

CHAPTER 16

THE NEW FOREST

To my eyes at least, there was always something of glamour to the way the Colonel did things. Although I still sparred and worked out in Jack's gym in Bournemouth, it was in the New Forest, under its awning of trees and watched by the royal deer, that I did my roadwork. Usually, if a trainer marshalled a boxer on his roadwork, especially during the winter months, he would protect himself against the cold with a woollen hat and roll-necked jumper. His transport was usually a bicycle and perhaps he would use a loud hailer, considering that volume would instil a sense of urgency in the tramping and tired pugilist. If nothing else it would break the monotony, heavy breathing and heavy footfalls.

I could not imagine the Colonel on a bicycle. Perhaps on the back of a tandem with Eric pedalling on the front, but the Colonel was not a person designed to use his own energy to get around. In replacement the Colonel had an ever-gleaming Ford Zephyr. Ensconced from the winter cold, not by woollens but by solid glass, he and Eric would follow me, permanently rolling forwards in first gear. Of course this effective protection also created a barrier between us. A loud hailer would have been useless. Instead we had a pre-devised routine involving pips of the horn, which would prompt me into changes of rhythm.

One toot and I would shadow box onwards, one-two, one-two, ducking and then weaving, avoiding imaginary punches, sending left and right hooks in symmetrical patterns through the sharp morning air. The second toot and I would pivot and run backwards with high knees, looking straight at the Colonel, his morning paper held low for a minute. Eric, his hands loosely on the wheel, watched out for the Colonel's instruction. Then the third toot and

I would sprint deer-like along the empty road and hear the Zephyr breathe up into second gear, never allowing a gap to open between us. Lastly the fourth, which would restore the monotonous pace and I would imagine the Colonel's paper rising again to block me from view. This was my daily morning routine in the first months of 1955 and I felt like I was jogging into universal eulogy and adoration.

Since the Colonel entered my life I had lost only three bouts and I had appeared on television. At that point I felt I could carry myself with a certain amount of swagger that was not just mere bravura. It was as if I had realised what my fate was to be and the swagger was justified. The training, the eating, the drinking, the meeting people, the confidence and opulence of life with the Colonel all rose to an apogee one evening in Great Yarmouth.

I stepped out of Jack Turner's Austin onto the seafront and made my way to the elegant hotel Eric had booked, glad to see the snubbed backend of Jack's car moving off. The Colonel had an undisguised loathing for Jack and with a directness that matched Jack's own, told him that he was not welcome. Len was standing across the road from the hotel as I arrived, he'd stepped out to watch the sea and have a cigarette. Len tolerated Jack good-humouredly. He said he'd known much worse and that he was harmless. The March wind was sharp, blowing in from the North Sea. Len reached out and pulled my half-open coat closed as he greeted me, telling me to keep my chest covered. He knew that the physical rigors of hard training could leave a boxer susceptible to even the most innocuous possibility of illness. Hard fighting can do that. An effect similar to all the hard driving on the engine of Jack's Austin, that eventually rebelled and left him stranded somewhere in rural Essex on his way back from Great Yarmouth.

In fighting terms this period began in Bournemouth against the Nigerian welterweight champion, Santos Martins, who was

Left: Paul King and Santos Martins

141

known as The Black Panther, a decade before it implied anything political. The event would have been notable for no other reason than the fact that my mother, putting aside her natural impulses, agreed to come to watch me box for only the second time in all my amateur and professional fights. However, by the time I entered the Drill Hall her seat was empty. Martins had entered before me and my mother had seen him disrobe. Horrified that I was to fight this sculptured and toned physique, she had fled, fearing that she would witness her son's death. Perhaps it was because he was black, which was unusual in British boxing, not to mention west-country life, in the early fifties. Maybe it was prescient; in a sport that has now witnessed dominance by black athletes, this was only my second bout against a black man. The first had been the charity event in Barnstaple against Jack Kofi, organised by Freddie Mills. I remember his words when I expressed unnatural fear at the African's appearance. "Paul, they've got two arms and two legs the same as you, and they can feel pain just the same as you." And I had proved it that night, banishing that un-empirical innocence.

I learnt after the fight that my doom-stricken mother had chained-smoked outside to calm herself. Inside, all my concentration was mobilised on the fiery Nigerian who I simply could not subdue. The fight swayed from corner to corner; Martins was like an incessant wind. If I seemed to throw him backwards with two accurate hooks, he would come back moments later just as strong. I remember Len saying to me, somewhere in the middle of the fight, that Martins' legs were giving no signs of weakening. I would take one round, then he would take the next and so on, until eight rounds were gone. It was exhausting. Outside my mother was told that her son was still alive.

Two weeks later I was in Dundee. I travelled up with Bobby Johnson from Plymouth, who I had fought and beaten a couple of

Right (left to right): Paul King, Alex Grant and Bobby Johnson

years previously, but who was part of the scene of boxers from the South West who all knew each other. Bobby was fighting on the undercard that night. This was his second trip to Scotland in as many months. Back in December he had fought my opponent, Jimmy Croll and I had tasked him with giving me insight into his style.

In 1955 it was long way from Bournemouth to Dundee and all the way there I had been ploughing away at a pack of chewing gum. When enough saliva had gathered in my mouth I spat it into a bottle. By the time we reached Northumberland my jaw was aching and there was no room left in the bottle, so Bobby had to stop the car and empty the gooey liquid onto the side of the road. I kept going all the way beyond the Forth Bridge. Len had taught me the technique as a way of losing the crucial increments of weight that would pull you under the limit. By the time of the weigh-in I was half a pound lighter than I had been on the south coast.

In Scotland both Bobby and I became the 'Englishmen'. Not due to our own patriotism, but because it was foisted upon us by the nationalistic Scots, not only in the local papers but in the fight programme and even the officials and hangers-on. Whereas in England I would be the 'West-Country Lad', or the 'Torquay Tornado', for the Scots we seemed to represent our whole nation. They didn't realise how much we actually resented it. The florid display they made of tartan and drums and bagpipes when Jimmy Croll entered, was the leavening that made the dough rise. Bobby had already been beaten by a Glaswegian, Rory McGregor and I was determined not to go the same way.

It was one of the unusual occasions when I found that anger mutated into successful boxing. It might have been chance, Croll's bad preparation, or an early hesitation from which he couldn't

Left (left to right): Bobby Johnson, Alex Grant, Paul King

recover, but I attacked him immediately with some stiff jabs and opened an adrenal gland somewhere in my body that never stopped pouring forth. He gamely attempted a comeback at the end of the first, but it was nothing. During the break I could hardly sit down, I was so eager to have the liberty of the ring once more. Almost immediately, Croll followed his sweat onto the canvas. This time he got up and with admirable toughness, he did the same the next three. However, four seconds, six, eight, eight again and finally ten, he was counted out on his fifth time on the floor.

But that wasn't the last time I would visit Caird Hall, Dundee that year. Twelve days after pulling Jimmy Croll's pants down in front of his own fans, I was in front of mine. It was my first fight in Torquay and finding an opponent was a particular farce. Originally it was to be Eric Billington, who I'd already boxed twice with each of us taking a victory, but he dropped out. Jack then arranged for Jackie Braddock to have a rematch after our fight the previous September, but injury forced him out too. So finally it was to be Dave Underwood from Plymouth, who was almost a local. Underwood was not the type of boxer to make me apprehensive about my first home bout. Despite having made a promising start, his pro boxing career had faltered badly and he'd endured an unimaginable nine fights without a win. In the fight before me however, he'd managed a narrow points victory that had given him renewed hope.

In Torquay his hopes were dashed. I completely dominated him and after the fourth round the referee called a halt to the bout and with it his career. He gave up after that. As for me, as I was the main attraction and due to the headlining fight being such a wisp of disappointment, I was herded into putting on an exhibition; a four round sparring session with an old friend, Kurt Ernst. I suppose I should have been flattered that I was in such demand, at least in Torquay, but I couldn't help playing my part grudgingly. This was my third fight in quick succession and not what I needed. I felt stuck in a rigorous machine that gave little let up. I realised

GEORGE GRANT'S PROMOTIONS present

BOXING

AIRD HALL, DUNDEE, MONDAY, 14th FEBRUARY, 1955

Doors Open 6.30 p.m.   Commence 7.30 prompt

10-Round International Welterweight Contest at 10 st. 9 lbs.

JIMMY CROLL
DUNDEE

JIMMY CROLL

versus

PAUL KING
TORQUAY

PAUL KING   Rated one of the best Welters in Great Britain

so OTHER OUTSTANDING INTERNATIONAL CONTESTS

gside, Organ Gallery & Front Balcony	Centre Area & Balcony	Centre Area & Back Balcony	Back Area	Gallery
10/6	7/6	5/-	3/6	2/6

10/6, 7/6, 5/- Bookable and Reserved.   3/6 and 2/6 Bookable

OKING OFFICES—GRANTS' PROMOTIONS, High Street, Dundee. Phone 6073.
GRANTS' PROMOTIONS, 1 Graham Place, Dundee. Phone 81285.
GRANTS' PROMOTIONS, 83 High Street, Arbroath. Phone 3588.

ALD PRESS, DUNDEE

more and more how the organisation of boxing was less concerned with quality, or even with the drama that poor boxing can offer, but more for the ring of the calculating machine as it made money from those who sought such things.

This was how I spent the month before the night in Great Yarmouth. A rapid progression of declining intervals between big nights. The period between fighting Underwood and sparring with Ernst was a paltry nine days compared to the fourteen between Martins and Croll and the twelve between Croll and Underwood. All this still seems an error in judgement from Jack Turner and against all boxing sense. Yet it must have provided momentum or a sense of desperation or something, it can't have been coincidence that carried me through and gave me the single most eminent night I ever had in a boxing ring.

Boswell St Louis, the British West Indies lightweight champion, had begun to establish himself on the British boxing circuit proper and previous to our bout had six straight wins on his record. He had a shrewd manager in Sam Burns, who kept him in the upper reaches of British welterweight boxing well into his age-assisted decline in the early sixties. Burns was a good man who knew how to treat his fighters well beyond the call of boxing affairs.

Despite my own victories, St Louis was fancied to continue his ascendancy within the home country and the bookies had him as favourite. Even though we were both in the field as contenders to the welterweight crown, with hindsight, defeat might have had the effect of convincing the promoters and press that I had exhausted my promise, as happens with so many boxers who are temporarily lauded. That is the nature of boxing much more than any other sport. Because winning is so highly prized, losing is often taken as an indication that the fury of the professional ring is not a safe place for many aspirants. Consequently, when a promoter or the press notice a young boxer who has the ability to win, they will exemplify him and offer up the expectation that he might become a contender. Almost every other sport can redeem a loss by the mere joy and satisfaction of competing. A losing boxer of healthy mind will look in the mirror and see the protrusions and divisions scattered across his face. In these he will see his only compensation, which can be one of two things: a paltry extra day off training, or an epiphany that he has laboured under a delusion and that he was not meant for the ring after all.

To be superstitious about place would not have served me favourably in Great Yarmouth that night, as I had fought at the Hippodrome before and lost. I had a distinct wariness before the fight, which seemed to be echoed in Len's strategy for the opening round. He advised me to move and to work behind my left hand, keeping away from Louis' formidable power. In the event, it was not a strategy I had any chance of maintaining. St Louis wasn't slow and I wasn't the boxer to be able to do that against boxers who aren't slow. I learned very fast that when I jabbed at him with my left, I had to follow it with a right or he would be on me. Yet by the opening minute, blood sluggishly came from his nose. Left jabs to the face, both fists in a barrage at his body and St Louis could not keep up. I was dominant. Then in the third, there was a moment, unexpected and heavy, when he caught me with a right-hook. I hadn't seen it coming and I lurched unbalanced, but did not fall. This was St Louis' highest speculation in a fight of thrift.

For his miserliness I blew up his ear. In the fifth he showed nothing and got uncounted lefts throwing him backwards into constant defence. Time after time he would try to fight back but I would pin him on the ropes and attempt to tunnel my way through his torso, so he would draw his guard downwards and I would score to his head. In the penultimate round he drew my blood also, a sliver of a cut across my brow. It was far too little to alter anything. What he did in the last round was much more significant. With the desperation of losing and the relief that even loss provides, often the boxer at the very end, begins to match his opponent. Some people call it pride. And for the final round that night, St Louis, effacing sentimentality, mastered himself and equalled me in punches. Not because he thought he had any chance of taking a decision, but because lasting to the end would give him a larger fee and because as he was hitting me, I couldn't hit him. He'd had enough of being punched for one night. So the crowd got their entertainment. Rung of everything vital but the sense of victory, the referee raised my right hand.

Exhaustedly, floating through the crowd, I heard Jack Turner talking to a journalist and shouting "Anytime! Anytime! We'll give him a return anytime!" He could pick up a bottle of milk and it would turn sour. After champagne, I lay in my room whilst the celebrations carried on without me. Before my ragged body was taken by sleep, I wondered if I would ever be so spectacular again.

CHAPTER 17

LONDON'S BRUTAL GRAVITY

The Levene International Star Boxing Tournament, 22nd March 1955, Empress Hall, Earls Court, organised by Harry Levene and raising funds for the Jewish Lads' Brigade. On the bill that evening: leading cruiserweight Ron Barton against, ex-light-heavyweight champion of Spain, Ramon Martinez; Blackpool's Brian London, one time challenger to Cassius Clay's world title, making his professional bow against Dennis Lockton; future European, Empire and British lightweight champion Dave Charnley versus Denny Dawson; soon to be Empire lightweight champion Kid Bassey touching gloves with Frenchman Marcel Ranvial; middleweight contender Lew Lazer facing Sharkey Lewis; and Paul King against the fates' champion, Peter Waterman, and his own imploding psyche.

There must be something greater to aim for in any sport, than to simply win a match or a bout. Any opposing notion was weeded out when people began to realise that sport could be a business. In boxing there are belts, otherwise known as titles, because fans and boxers alike need to know who is the best fighter. So a complex spider web of entanglement was devised, one that gives certain boxers the opportunity to prove that they are that man, because all boxers strive to be the best.

There was a ruling trinity of London prize-fighting in the 1950s; Harry Levene, Jarvis Astaire and Jack Solomons, a boxing society more insular than any in the provinces. This percolated all the way down to the fans, who considered themselves to be the only true pugilistic aficionados. They bought tickets for fights, not only so they could be entertained by athleticism and fascinated by the struggle of wills, but also to sit as jury, ready to dispense their superior judgement. For those of us outside the metropolis, London was a fast moving current of snobbery and nepotism. If Levene was organising and promoting Waterman and Astaire managing him, the only one missing was Jack Solomons, who I was sure would be somewhere providentially affecting proceedings, in the absence of any direct physical involvement.

This was not the first time I had been within a set of ropes with Peter Waterman. It was in the summer of 1952. I had been unbeaten in my first twelve professional fights and was supplementing my income at the Penzance fair. A telegram arrived from Jarvis Astaire, delivered by the police, as if it was from the Lord Chief Justice summoning me to the Old Bailey. The telegram instructed me to go to London because Astaire wanted me to be a sparring partner for his protégé, Waterman. Whatever injustice there was in London's dominance of the boxing world, it would have been perhaps honourable but nevertheless suicide, to have snubbed him. Not that this was even a consideration at the time. I was content to comply and accept the excellent wage Astaire offered me. Coming out of a situation where most of my training was done on a boxing booth, I felt like a man suffering from famine being called to dine at a table of plenty. I was just in time to catch the last train before the 1952 rail strike locked down the nation's standard gauges.

Astaire knew his business well and like a man of finance who reads the fluctuations of the market every morning, he was an assiduous follower of the professional boxing results. He was aware that I was unbeaten and in his natural condescension to country-bred boys, thought that I would be good material to help Waterman, who had recently returned from the Helsinki Olympics, prepare for his first professional bout. Three years later I proved myself competent enough to be let into the ring with him, accompanied by that essential third part of a boxing match: a referee.

Not that I had any cynicism about the concentration of boxing power in the capital in 1952, I was full of naive opportunism and deference. This was only natural in the presence of such luminous names as Danny Holland and Snowy Buckingham at the Thomas à Beckett pub on the Old Kent Road, a place that was as saturated in boxing as it was in alcohol. Buckingham and Holland, despite the sordid politics of the London prize-ring, maintained a pureness of spirit and were concerned with the artistry and labour of boxing above all else.

When I first met Waterman, the self-confidence of his character betrayed that in his mind he already wore the regal robes of a champion. He wasn't alone in thinking these thoughts and around him there had formed a coterie, who were made to feel the privilege of their proximity and acted dutifully sycophantic. Not that he or they were wrong of course, he did take the British and the European welterweight titles. I watched the goings on of the gym with curiosity. Waterman was never great, not nearly great, but his vanity was attractive in a vicarious way and to a certain extent I empathised with his arrogance. However, the certainty with which he had been groomed, simply because they of London felt themselves the holders of all vitality, was the first inclination I had that boxing wasn't, as sports should be, solely concerned with talent and desire.

By the time I was to meet Waterman at Earls Court, he was like I had been back in 1952: unbeaten. Telegrams, letters and cards began to arrive at Highcliffe in the weeks leading up to the bout. They were redirected from a variety of places, because the Colonel always insisted on the privacy of our address. The majority were full of optimism from fans, friends and acquaintances, all seeking to endow me with good luck and expressing their sincerest hopes that I could mangle Waterman. A few were worded angrily and it was these that concerned me the most. The ill will they bore seemed to me portentous of disaster. After I had read them I would immediately throw them away, superstitious of any curse they may bring.

The press, no doubt roused by the fastidiousness of Mickey Duff, who was amongst Waterman's camp as a promoter, covered the fight with comprehensive previews. One of the stories he had fed them dredged up the story of a two-decade old rivalry. The fight was ludicrously billed as a replay of the Len Harvey and Larry Gains rivalry from the 1930s. Larry Gains had apparently been visiting Waterman's gym, and in his own era had twice challenged Len for the Empire belt and twice been repulsed. Len held no grudge and it seems unlikely that Larry felt anything other than respect for one of his fellows who he had met in combat all those years ago. I think it was something that Duff and the paper men would have called an angle, or a way to put bums on seats; a desperate attempt to wring as much money from the fight as they could.

One evening before the fight I read an opinion piece written by Freddie Mills, even though the Colonel had advised me not to. In it he had blustered about how interesting it would be to see if Waterman's boxerly skills could stand up to my power and ferocity. However, there was a statement that followed, which was the only sentence anyone was interested in 'I must fancy Waterman'. Reading it I remembered his baleful predictions before my Southern Area title fight against Terry Ratcliffe, in which Mills had backed my opponent and the eventual winner, and my mood dropped for the night.

In the time leading up to the Waterman fight it became more and more obvious that the Colonel was feeling uneasy with his itinerant lifestyle. It was as if age, which had always seemed something irrelevant, was involuntarily reigning him in. He seemed to find it extremely difficult to put into simple words and say to me directly that he was moving back to his ancestral lands in Scotland, taking Eric with him of course. But I knew it, and

TO RAISE FUNDS FOR THE JEWISH LADS BRIGADE

Harry Levene Presents

INTERNATIONAL

BOXING

AT THE

ROYAL ALBERT HALL

RON BARTON
(West Ham)

S. 22nd MAR. 1955

RAMON MARTINEZ
(Spain)

OFFICIAL PROGRAMME **2/-**

despite his vagueness, that he wanted me to go with them. I was unsure how much or how little strained finances were the true motivation, but I always thought that this was an easier and more palatable excuse, that served to obscure the real reasons, which were perhaps more complex than he could ever say. However, the move was certain and I was certain that I couldn't go with them. The isolation would have been too great and the aura of retirement too stultifying for me as a boxer, which was an idea that I still had passion for, being only twenty-three.

Mental preparation for a fight is the most difficult thing to control. It requires a religious temperament of complete faith to uphold and so many different concerns can weigh upon it. When I was with my Bournemouth landlady frequent sex wasn't enough to take it out of me physically, but the fear of disaster from mixing copulation and pugilism was enough to unseat me psychologically. It was impossible to blame the Colonel for a taking a decision concerning his own life, but the belief and hope that his patronage had given me, to witness that begin to ebb away was like fighting a battle knowing that even after victory you will weaken into submission. The optimism that I had begun to generate again, with the defeats of Jimmy Croll, Dave Underwood and Boswell St Louis, was now negated. The opulence of life with the Colonel always reached its highest pitch before a fight but it felt almost like an elegy when we checked into the Richmond Hill Hotel prior to the Waterman bout. The splendour of that evening was as much as I had experienced from boxing in the 1950s. The luxury of the dressing rooms with padded benches and unspoilt rows of coat hooks, the magnitude of the arena heaving with people and lit up so that the ring glowed like a luminescent planetary ring. Yet any last hopes that the sense of occasion could rouse me to victory, were brilliantly crushed by the calamitous double act of Jack Turner and my father.

Turner's mere presence in the dressing room, accompanied, as he always was, by the reek of alcohol was enough to depress me. It was a reminder that apart from my cheerleader Len Harvey, Jack's one-eyed, red face was all that would advocate for my future career. My father sometimes used sentiment to get a free ticket ringside and sit as part of my team. A venue as big as Earls Court was not one he was going to miss. These two bookended the procession to the ring; Jack led, followed by Len, then myself and then my father.

We navigated the steps that led up to a precipice, enclosed within the seating area, which led downwards again towards the ring. Security was usually limited to a few policemen at entrances and exits and it was common to see staff, press, officials, any number of people loitering about the corridors in the underbelly of stadiums. As we wound our way from the dressing room several people patted me and wished me good luck. I noticed a man leaning against the wall and I thought that he was going to do the same. He let Jack and Len pass and then visciously but not loudly, he spat "You're fucking lucky". I was surprised and stopped, even though I knew I shouldn't. I shouldn't even have heard him, but my mind was not focussed. He went on "In Bristol, that time, when that nutter jumped in the ring, he wasn't no mad Scotsman, it was your father. I could have lost you your licence for that. You owe just being here..." and then he was cut off.

He was wrong that it wasn't a mad Scotsman who had jumped in the ring, my father was indeed Scottish and on occasion, acted in a way that would not be inaccurate to call mad. The incident the man referred to had happened, but if he had been there, he obviously hadn't remembered my father's face. There was no hesitation, my father held me aside with one hand and slammed the other straight into his unsuspecting face. The man fell and his head sharply cracked against the steps. The sound wasn't unusual, but knowing where it came from endowed it with a sickening horror. Blood gushed out, cascading down the steps, a stream chasing us towards the ring. My father pushed me forwards over the man's unconscious body, sucking his knuckles.

Royal Albert Hall

Doors Open
6.30 p.m.

TUESDAY, 22nd MARCH

Commence
7.30 p.m.

HARRY LEVENE presents
International Star Boxing Tournament to raise Funds
for THE JEWISH LADS' BRIGADE.

10 (3-Min.) Rounds International Contest at 12st. 9lb.

RON   RAMON
BARTON v MARTINEZ

Leading Contender for the
Cruiserweight Championship.

Ex-Light-Heavyweight Champion of
Spain, drew with Charles, Colin,
French champion.

---

8 (3-Min.) Rounds International Contest at 9st. 2lb.

Hogan BASSEY v Marcel RANVIAL

(Nigeria)   (France)

Professional Debut of Great Britain's Sensational Amateur
Heavyweight Champion. 6 (3-Min.) Rounds Contest.

Brian LONDON v Dennis LOCKTON

(Blackpool)   (Manchester)

---

8 (3-Min.) Rounds Contest at 9st. 4lb.

DAVE CHARNLEY v DENNY DAWSON

(Dartford). Undefeated   Central Area Featherweight
Champion

---

8 (3-Min.) Rds. Contest at 10st. 9lb.	8 (3-Min.) Rds. Contest at 11st. 8lb.
# Peter WATERMAN	# LEW LAZAR
(Clapham). Undefeated. V	Aldgate). V
# PAUL KING	# Kit POMPEY
(Torquay).	(Gold Coast).

---

6 (3-Min.) Rounds Contest at 12st 8lb.

JACK LONDON Jnr.   v   EDDIE WRIGHT
(Blackpool)   (Mile End)

Prices 63s. 42s. 30s. 21s. 15s. 10/6 7/6

Tickets from: Harry Levene Promotions, Albany Club, Savile Row,
W.1. (REG 7382). Royal Albert Hall (KEN 8212) and agents.

Len had heard the crack and although he hadn't seen the altercation, he looked round in anger at my father. It had all been enacted beyond the view of the crowd and they were blessedly ignorant. There I was, in my beautiful red gown, the golden characters of 'Torquay' embroidered on the back, about to face the most stylish welterweight in the country. Shamefully, my father had reduced the occasion to the sordid brutality and lowliness of a cheap punch laid on an unguarded man. But I was more forlorn than furious; it seemed just another inevitable aspect of this doomed night, useless to try and rectify or make any sense out of it. I caught a glimpse of Jarvis Astaire traversing the ringside and heading for the steps that led toward the changing rooms. In those few moments I began to wonder if I was watching a great puppeteer, calmly and dispassionately going to assess the damage to one of his marionettes. Could it have been? Or was I merely interpreting shadows? Just before the bell was rung, he was back by Waterman's corner. Jack's alcoholic fumes drifted across my face, they smelt almost sweet this time, a reminder that something soothing lay beyond. I didn't listen to a word he said. Len stoically gripped my shoulder, gave me one last good luck and climbed through the ropes. Then my legs extended automatically, as if hoisted by strings and the clapper struck three times.

Perhaps I had seen and heard enough of violence, perhaps I wanted it over quickly and without all the bluster of ignominious struggle, but I did try to box Waterman. In the first two rounds I managed it, but they were unspectacular and tentative. Waterman was probably waiting for me to begin my predictable fury in earnest, waiting for me to expose a weakness with my impatience. By the end of the first it would have been difficult to say who had the round. By the end of the second the judges would have had to act on prejudice to call it other than a draw and I found myself with renewed hope. In the corner Jack was at me to go after Waterman, telling me that I was here to box not dance.

Danny Holland, that fine corner and cuts man, had told me in the lead up to the fight that the reason Waterman had so many early round victories on his card was because he knew how to exploit his boxing licence's limits. It was a combination that he had down to perfection, but it needed a moment of certainty, because to fail could leave him off balance and defenceless. The move, as Holland described it, was a jab with the left immediately followed by a right, throwing his whole body behind it, so that if the right missed, the head wouldn't. In the third round Waterman must have seen his moment of certainty and took his chance. I managed to block the left, but the right didn't miss and neither did the head. The strings that held up my legs went slack and the skin across my brow split apart.

But I got up. I was in that period of uncertainty, when it is impossible to know how bad the cut is and whether another blow would rip your feet from underneath you interminably. If I had boxed with arrogance rather than awe and a sense of futility, I might have attacked him as if in revenge. Had I done so, it would have been a better form of self-preservation than weaving and ducking, blocking and backing my way towards the bell. It was not in my instinct to do that, yet I did it, and I made myself look as if I'd had enough punishment and enough boxing. It had been a mistake, the whole fight a mistake. The implacable pessimism, strange in those who have worked so hard to get there, was like a contagious pestilence in my corner and the referee seemed to want to be rid of it. He came over as I sat on the stool and said, with mannerly authority that the fight was over; he could see that I wanted no more. But it was all mistake.

CHAPTER 18

THERE'S NO BUSINESS LIKE SHOW BUSINESS

"Why do you do it, Paul? Most people try to avoid getting knocked about and yet you do it for a living." Her name was Jane, an actress of innumerable parts, supporting roles to actors who had names on a poster, swelling a scene or two. They were all like that, ensconced in a Victorian labyrinth on Churchill Road, Bournemouth, striving for recognition. It could have been my own thoughts, projected through the mouth of a beautiful girl and delivered as though written by a great tragedian. "Ever played charades?" I asked, but none of them ever understood.

In the dressing room after the fight, Jarvis Astaire bounced in with a great grin, mooning at me, like a murderer turning up at the wake of his victim. My apathy and exhaustion allowed him to be welcomed, but this was his town and he was welcome anywhere. He told me that I'd done well; he lied. Luck was a greater force in this game than people gave it credit for, he told me. I told him that my legs were fine and stood up and I asked him if he could see my cut. He knew, he knew, he told me and called me son. Like he said: Luck. Like losing money that is impossible to recover and the mad scramble of the mind for places where it might be found. I knew I had failed my big chance, and I knew I just had myself to blame; the Colonel, Jack, my Father, Jarvis, Harry Levene, Jack Solomons, none of them could be held responsible for my defeat. I asked Jarvis if I'd get my rematch. "You'll get a return. Don't worry." Then he left, dragging all my possibilities with him. As he opened the door I could hear the tumult of celebration down the corridor in Waterman's dressing room.

Later that evening in the hotel, the Colonel poured out four fingers of whisky and handed it to me. Len told me not to worry, I had just fought the wrong fight. I told The Colonel what Astaire had said about my rematch, but in the periphery of my vision I could see Len looking at the Colonel with a face that spoke of reality. It spoke with experience and it said I had no chance.

I met the actor Jimmy Malborne through Johnny Sullivan, the British middleweight champion from Preston who I sparred with, earning three pounds a day. I was staying at Sullivan's house, always preferring home comforts to the impersonal cleanliness of a hotel. Jimmy was also lodging with Sullivan as he was performing at the local theatre. Both being strangers to the town made Jimmy and I good friends and we stayed in touch. When my subsequent fight after Waterman, against Santos Martins, was arranged in Torquay, he was in town with a production and came to see me perform. Afterwards, over a drink, we got talking and arrived on the subject of the departing Colonel and my impending homelessness. Jimmy said that he had a few friends in Bournemouth who lodged in a huge Victorian house that would be perfect for me and cheap, because most of the people who lived there had more hope than money. Apparently they were wealthy in curiosity and understanding and, he said with a wink, were about as liberal as anyone wanted. Perhaps actors make the best salesmen.

"Isn't anyone playing a boxer?" I asked. But no one ever was. There were singers, actors, comedians, actor/comedians, singer/actors, singer/comedians, actor/singer/comedians, but none ever played the part of a boxer, except me. They were in variety, serious drama, comedy, theatres, workingmen's clubs and the backrooms of pubs on makeshift stages. They toured, they played the same venue for weeks, they dreamed of television and the West End, or Hollywood and Broadway and then they grew older and began to see the moments when they had missed their opportunity.

If I needed the toilet in the night, or a glass of water from the kitchen, walking down the corridors was always like walking into a Brian Rix Whitehall farce. A strip of light would appear along the wall, a head would split it in two before retreating and shutting the door behind it. If the head was already in the corridor it would mutter a tactful "evening" and then retreat, or face the wall, hat pulled down. Sometimes these mysterious heads would come from actress's rooms, sometimes from actors'. They were invariably older men: agents, theatre managers, production managers, directors and, according to their taste, they would be getting favours in exchange for preferential treatment. It was talent needing power; I knew their like in boxing.

On the 5th of June 1956, Peter Waterman faced Wally Thom at Harringey and stopped him in the fifth to become British welterweight champion. On the 14th of January 1958, Peter Waterman climbed into the ring for the second time against Emilio Marconi. Previously they had drawn in Rome, after fifteen rounds. In London, in his return bout, Waterman knocked Marconi out in the fourteenth and he became European welterweight champion. I read it on the back pages of a national.

"You're making a right cunt of yourself," followed a rich draft of alcohol-laden air. I was in Torquay, the town hall sold out and Santos Martins, from Nigeria, was on top after four rounds; I'd been down twice already. "And in front of your home fans too!" For once I agreed with Jack Turner. These were not the snobbish fans of London, most of whom were as eager to see a failure as a champion. Loyalty was above any cynicism for my fans, and I believed that I owed them something. It was most unlikely that any had come to support Martins. So, at the beginning of the fifth, rising from my self-imposed adversity and self-pitying self-destruction, I blasted Martins, be-ruffled him and chased him all over the ring until his plume was colourless. I won a close points decision.

After the fight I met up with Jimmy, actor friend to fighters, and we talked over kindred troubles. I quite fancied one of the girls who had a room on the corridor above mine but Jimmy's wife had warned me not to get involved. She had told me that the girl was a part-time hostess. It meant nothing to me until I spoke to Jack about it. In his forthright and unsympathetic way, he laughed "What she really means is, the bird's a whore. Well, they usually are those theatrical types" he reasoned.

Because of my friendships I used to get free tickets to see the big acts when they came to the Hippodrome in Bournemouth. Eve Boswell, Alma Cogan, Frankie Vaughan and comedians like Dave King, I went to see them all. I offered my housemates the same in kind, but they were all baffled by my business and none of them ever came to see me fight.

Jarvis Astaire, in the underbelly of the Empress Hall, had spoken to me of luck, thinking that I knew no better. It seemed that most of my theatrical friends indeed knew no better; they all spoke of this immaterial force that would snatch them up and parachute them onto the stages or set of a big production. One particular night at the Hippodrome seemed to confirm this for them. A girl who lived in our house, was performing in the chorus when an impresario who was holidaying on the coast spotted her. After the show he signed her up and within two days her room was empty and she was gone. It seemed for show business, as much for fight business, that life was located north east of Hampshire. The lucky girl, spotted on the Hippodrome stage, had gone to London.

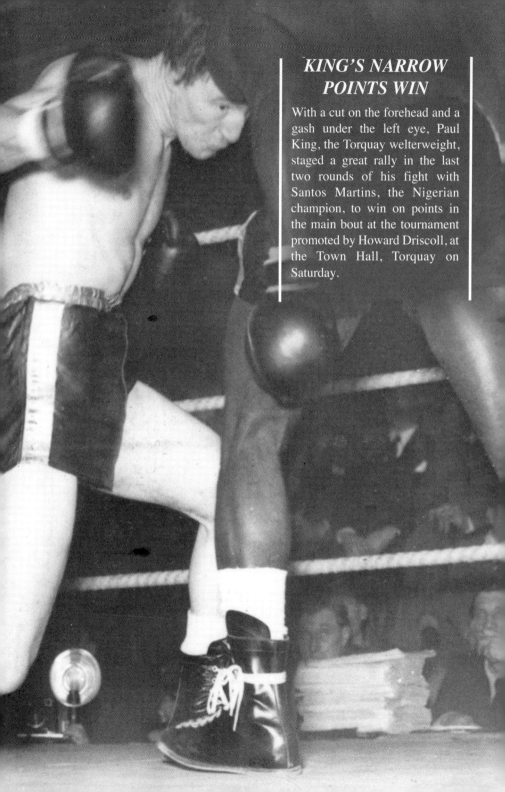

KING'S NARROW POINTS WIN

With a cut on the forehead and a gash under the left eye, Paul King, the Torquay welterweight, staged a great rally in the last two rounds of his fight with Santos Martins, the Nigerian champion, to win on points in the main bout at the tournament promoted by Howard Driscoll, at the Town Hall, Torquay on Saturday.

CHAPTER 19

THOMAS À BECKET, 1955

Soon after the Santos Martins fight I received a second summons from Jarvis Astaire to go to London. As a result of the Colonel's departure, I had returned to Bournemouth to resume my training regime with Jack Turner. So when Astaire requested my presence at the Thomas à Becket to help spar some of his boys, I felt it was prudent to accept. Not because his desires were not to be disobeyed, but because staying in Bournemouth seemed like hiding out in the woods. Somehow, going back to London, the site of defeat, made it easier to go on boxing. Plus three pounds per round was better than window cleaning. Of course Waterman would be there. The Becket was his base and Astaire his manager. Perhaps that's what Astaire intended our rematch to be: simply a sparring one.

The whole gamut of the boxing world could be found above that pub on the Old Kent Road. Young, green hopefuls who were the promise of the next generation. Bucket and sponge men who would tell anyone, no matter if they listened or not, how they were there twenty years ago in the corner of some half-remembered champion's night of glory. There were also the time trialled journeymen who couldn't or wouldn't get out soon enough and still lingered. Champions and contenders like Waterman or Yolande Pompey and the men with all the knowledge but not the ability or youth to put it into practice themselves, who instead showed those who were able how. And of course, the power brokers and money-men who controlled the game and stalked about in suits having deigned a brief visit on their charges.

I wasn't always required at the Becket and found myself flitting between London and Bournemouth. I was in constant training, paid for in London yet having to clean windows in Bournemouth. Throughout this time Jack continued to organise any fight that would earn him money, and so it was that I found myself in St Austell, Cornwall.

Fighting was not Rees Moore's forte and it came as an expected let down from Jack to be told that the Welshman, who I had beaten twice already, was to be my next opponent. Boxing was just a job, but Rees Moore made it a boring one. He ran; I chased him; he grabbed me and the referee called it a draw. Jack had three of us who were on the same bill in St Austell; a nice little earner for him.

Then it was back to the Becket. Joe Lucy was the landlord at the time, an ex-lightweight champion, who still liked to get between the ropes occasionally. He'd come and watch the training and sometimes coax me into giving him a couple of rounds. Danny Holland would laugh and then, because he couldn't help himself, shout instructions at us both. A great trainer, Danny had once been a significant prospect from the amateurs until he badly hurt his back working on the wharves. He was training Henry Cooper, who was always at the Becket. Other gyms like Kline's on the Tottenham Court Road, for all their excellence in the practicalities of boxing training, never had the aura of the Becket. It was like a shrine, a place of pilgrimage; full of fighting folklore, from direct memory and ancient tales that had been passed between London's pugilists for half a century or more. I wish I had recorded some of them or could remember better. Boxers would nudge me and whisper to look at someone, then tell me a name that would echo somewhere in remembrance of boxing's history.

For most of the boxers back then, fighting was not their whole lives, even if it had their hearts. As time moved on, necessity would always bite. Many would come back to the Becket for a drink, to watch the young boxers and envy them. Amongst those young boxers who trained at the Becket in 1955 were Sammy

McCarthy; who had by then lost his featherweight crown to Spider Kelly; Terry Spinks, who was still a seventeen year old amateur and had yet to win Olympic gold; and Dave Charnley, who was European, Commonwealth and British lightweight champion in his time. Even though he was a lightweight I was glad I never had to spar with Charnley. The Dartford Destroyer certainly knew how to punch and punch fast, I wouldn't have welcomed having to keep up with him.

However, on one occasion, I did spar with Yolande Pompey. He was a huge light-heavyweight from Trinidad and renowned as a big hitter. Danny Holland approached me, explaining that Pompey's sparring partner hadn't turned up and would I be prepared to step in. Danny was just too nice to refuse. As I stepped into the ring I distinctly remember him saying, "Just move him about a bit, Paul." And move I did, there was no stopping me. If I had stood still there was the likely chance that I would have been vibrating in my boots. Nevertheless it was fun, even if I didn't get paid. The following year Pompey had a shot at the world championship in Harringey, against that Mississippian magician Archie Moore. Pompey lost, but it was a monumental night of boxing to have witnessed; I was on the undercard that night.

Not too long after the third Moore fight I was boxing in Bournemouth. No one from Churchill Road turned up, but the town hall was full anyway; apparently the show at the Hippodrome that night wasn't up to much. And for a while against Dennis Read I didn't think I was; he rattled me with sharp right-handers and cut me in the last round but I got the points decision, narrowly. My cut stopped me from helping out at the Thomas à Becket for a while and in the intervening period I moved out of the old Victorian mansion. Although the strangeness of my house-mates had been a salve after the disappointment of losing to Waterman, my sister, Edna, moved to Bournemouth to begin training as a nurse and we decided to share a flat together. It was at this time one of my strangest fights occurred.

"I'm to take you up to London to fight Albert Carroll." The man was in the driving seat of a large Daimler parked outside my flat. I asked him how much. "Seventy." I thought of the twelve pounds I made cleaning windows each week. Then I thought of the complete absence of any preparation. I had been training, but not as intensively as I normally would have been in the build-up to a fight. I thought of the seventy pounds, I thought of my record, I thought of the money. My sister came for the ride. It was obvious what had happened; Jack. When *Boxing News* reported the fight afterwards they said that I had endured a five hour car ride from Devon in order to stand in. If that was the perception then I was happy with it, as it gave a mitigating factor to anyone who might query the loss. And a loss it was, but nothing close to the humiliation I had contemplated on the journey up.

I had troubled Carroll throughout with my big punches. Reasoning that my relative lack of fitness would be a major drawback, I stolidly claimed the centre of the ring and aimed constant hulking blows at his body, giving up my usual chasing game. But this had its disadvantages. Carroll was quick and his fast feet often caused my punches to miss wide of the mark. His retaliation was tough and he used both fists well, but a quote from the subsequent *Boxing News* report has always been one of my favourites: 'As the fight progressed King took his rival's punches with disdain'. It suggests that I was sneering at the sport and its trials, whilst exploiting its money-making potential. That is how I like to remember that fight, like a robbery. With less than a minute before the final bell, and an inevitable points decision for Carroll, I sunk my finest left hook into his body and he fell. I was there, behind the referee in a neutral corner, willing him to stay down, hoping that a victory would be registered as disdain for the sport that offers hope and glory and then brutally mangles it. To the credit of Carroll's will power he drew himself up unsteadily and survived the remaining few seconds which was, in the opinion of *Boxing News*, 'astonishing'.

CHAPTER 20

THE ITALIAN JOB

If the job offers benefits, then take them. Back training at the Becket one day, Snowy Buckingham called me over and said that I was wanted on the telephone. It was Jack. He said that he had managed to get me a fight in Bologna. Dundee was the furthest I had ever travelled. He said that the pay was good and when I asked how much he said seven hundred pounds, ten times the amount for fighting Albert Carroll. It was hard to believe, especially coming from Jack. Cynical as he had made me, I expected a drawback, possibly the journey. I imagined myself hitch-hiking across Europe with peasants in donkey carts passing me. As I said: Dundee.

When the travel arrangements arrived it was as if I was an international assassin. Jack told me to go to an Italian restaurant in Cambridge Circus and look for a man wearing a black hat and black suit with a red rose in the lapel. This is when I began to think that Jack had organised some elaborate hoax in order to humiliate me. Nevertheless, I went to the restaurant, where there were numerous men wearing black suits. The hat stand at the entrance hadn't a peg free for another black hat. I glanced around the room and couldn't see anyone with a dash of crimson across their breast. Thankfully this was not espionage and Jack had supplied me with the man's name. This left me to discretely inquire at each table if Nick Cavelli was amongst their company. After about the fourth table the man himself overheard his name being bandied about and without the effusiveness stereotypical to Italians, he motioned me over and introduced himself.

Fortunately that was as bad as it got. Cavelli accompanied me to London airport where we boarded a flight to Milan. The journey certainly didn't live up to my fears and from an unreal beginning this was slowly becoming the most glamorous event of my boxing career. You have to understand that commercial flying was still young and the huge majority of people had not yet taken to the skies. So flying to Italy, because it was so unusual, was a small adventure in itself.

The first night we stayed in Milan; Cavelli went out, I went to bed. The following morning we ate breakfast and had a stroll around before making our way to Milan's grand and impressive train station, where we took a train to Bologna. Pictures of Mussolini and his fellow fascists hung from meat hooks around the square in the city centre. This was where we met up with Uber Bacilieri, who became heavyweight champion of his country. He was on the bill that night, in between two fights in England against Henry Cooper. Perhaps the same connections that organised his English fights also organised my Italian one. He showed us around the city and would break out in a baritone whenever the moment suggested it. He told me that if he hadn't been a boxer he would have been an opera singer.

The weigh-in surprised me. In England all the fighters and their trainers would usually mill about quite informally, and often we would be naked. In Bologna we had an audience: pressmen and fans sat in the tiered cinema and observed the ceremony. When it came to my turn I began to hear heckles of, 'Inglese!' I thought I heard them ask for a good view, so I turned my back on them and bent over. They roared with laughter and I was hustled onto the scales by the scandalised Italian officials. It was only here, at the weigh-in that I found out who I was to be fighting. His name was Luigi Coluzzi and he was a contender for the Italian title.

I spoke to a couple of Italian journalists and was impressed that they knew my record almost as well I did. However, after the initial surprise and pleasure at being the object of curiosity, their knowledge cast a momentary dark shadow over what had been, up until then, a trip of forgetfulness. I was forced to recall how, even though I had only nine losses to my name, I had failed whenever there had been an opportunity to break out from the ranks of mediocrity. The flying, the foreign cities, the operatic heavyweights, the money, had all blinded me to the disappointment of the stalling progress of my career. There was nothing greater to strive for now, no notion of glory and history and I had begun to accept and even like it like that. So I shook off the journalists' unintended sobering of my mood and resolved to enjoy myself as much as possible.

I had an early meal followed by the greatest bowl of ice cream I had ever eaten. Then I went happily through the warmth of the Italian evening with Cavelli to the Palazzo Della Sport. It was some bill that night. Hometown boy Franco Cavicchi was defending the European heavyweight title against the German, Heinz Neuhaus, whom he had won it from and who had since then beaten him in a non-title bout. They were of course the main attraction, but there were some other great fighters to watch, such as Tiberio Mitri who had lost a World middleweight title bout to Jake LaMotta, but who was the European champion and who would defend it against Randy Turpin. Also Emilio Marconi, whose European welterweight belt Peter Waterman would take at the second attempt.

We had an hour's wait in the dressing room whilst Bacilieri and others fought out the early preliminaries. Ours was to be the final fight before the main contest. Although the build-up had been a happy one, the preparations were as serious as ever and I had to work hard to build up my mood. Finally the knock on the door came and Cavelli and I made our way along the corridor with plenty of excitable Italians forming a train behind us, chattering in their own language. Soon I couldn't hear them at all. The noise from the crowd was funnelled down the corridor and enveloped everything around us. Sixty thousand people were waiting.

The fight began, we boxed; I returned to my corner. I asked Cavelli his opinion of the fight so far. He replied that Coluzzi had an insurmountable lead on points and that I had been down twice. Consternated at his reply I asked what round the last one had been. He told me it was the seventh. What had happened, I don't know. I knew I had been boxing, but it was as if in my mind time had contracted itself so that I felt only a single round had passed. That bout of temporary amnesia has always remained a mystery. Writing this I can remember, with the type of memory that a lot of alcohol provides, being on the canvas and bouncing back up straight away, although I still can't say for certain whether it was once or twice. I simply couldn't explain what happened to my mind or why it happened. I could only conjecture, thinking it must have been the crowd or the Italian food. Cavelli said that I had been unresponsive between rounds and having never seconded for me before, he let it go, assuming that was how I worked.

I might have been down twice but it certainly didn't feel like it. I attacked Coluzzi with a vigour that must have surprised him and certainly came out on top in the closing rounds. He had however, like Cavelli had told me, an insurmountable lead and it was only pride and my unquenchable good humour that made me do it. In the last round I even caught him with a massive left hook, my speciality, and had him hanging off the ropes. The crowd was raucous at my comeback, thrilled despite their own man getting knocked about.

After the bell I did a handspring across the ring to show my freshness, because the Italians loved the showmanship. My face was quite badly cut over both eyes and on the bridge of my nose, but I didn't notice it until later. When the referee announced Coluzzi as the winner I was shocked as he came over to my corner, planted a kiss on each cheek and presented me with a bouquet of flowers. To show my humility and my regard for the occasion I raised Coluzzi's arm and drew another cheer from the excitable

174

Feeding the pigeons, Bologna, 1955

crowd. I was as happy at the end as I had been at the start. The display of respect and admiration from the Italians was beautiful.

Back in the dressing room I realised that my face was quite badly cut, but not even that seemed to matter. Cavelli said that there was a party organised for everyone involved in the night so I rested a little, cleaned up, had my wounds primed for healing and then we took a taxi. It was all alfresco. A meal with exotic

Italian food (I had never seen pasta before), speeches in an incomprehensible language, Heinz Neuhaus forcing a beer upon me and asking if I thought he could beat Henry Cooper and a beautiful Italian girl who pleaded with me to take her back to England. But I had a train to catch in the bright Bologna morning. No plane this time, just a long journey tied to the tracks through France and a windy ferry across the Channel.

Gone were the few fleeting days in Italy. Afterwards, the money and novelty of going to Italy overwhelmed the reason I was actually there. Nobody asked me much about the boxing, not even Len or Jack. Sometimes I felt as if it had never happened. But I would look again at the picture of myself and Uber Bacilieri, ready to burst into opera, feeding the pigeons in a renaissance piazza, to convince myself that it hadn't all been a dream.

CHAPTER 21

THE CAFÉ ROYAL

Heavy smoke billowed throughout the compact room; cloudlets puffed anonymously from within the hushed neat ranks of unbroken, uniform dinner suits, massed around the ring. I could even hear the polite suck as another draw was taken on a cigar. Between rounds discussions began as the spectators exchanged, sometimes with the fighters, their views on what was happening. This was the National Sporting Club, offering evenings of fine food and fine fighting all in the unspeakably opulent surroundings of the Café Royal, Regent Street, Piccadilly. An odd throwback of pretentious decorum forbade the crowd from any expression during the time that the boxers were in the ring. It was almost as if they regarded the two half-naked men in the middle of the room, examples of barbarism and themselves as the proprietors of civilisation, safely and voyeuristically entertained. Perhaps they thought that any hint of being excited by the spectacle before them would cause them to be tainted by the regressive behaviour, which they had paid to see and were obviously enjoying.

Since the turn of the century, the National Sporting Club had been the *de facto* governing body of boxing in Britain. It garnered patronage from the aristocracy; the Marquess of Queensbury was an early member and it offered Lonsdale belts, one in each weight category. The belts were introduced by the Earl of Lonsdale, a name that was subsequently passed on to the boxing clothing company. The British Board of Boxing Control assumed its role by the early 1930s, Lonsdale belts and all, and it vanished until wealthy men decided to put on their most exclusive costumes and watch it with unnatural restraint whilst devouring the finest cigars. The Café Royal had it's own history, displayed on the ceilings and walls. It seems odd now and it felt odd then, but we

Cafe Royal

London, W.1

boxed under the light of a shimmering chandelier that was shrouded in smoke. In the audience were celebrities, aristocracy and the very pinnacle of self-made men. Plenty had cigars, as if plain old cigarettes were not decorous enough and nearly all had some kind of short in a glass.

But before we boxed the members had their dinner. The set menu for the evening consisted of smoked Scottish salmon, or honeydew melon to start, Norfolk roast turkey with chestnut stuffing and cranberry sauce; fillet of grilled beef, tomatoes, mushrooms and fried onions; or steak, kidney and game pie for a main, and since the season was drawing close, Christmas pudding enflamed in brandy, or mince pies. But the real dessert was a light showering of blood and sweat, if you were lucky.

The wealthy are rarely generous and a boxer's experience of the Café Royal was quick and regimented. We were offered nothing from their vast kitchens except water. We were quick into the ring and then quick out of the building when we had finished and told that payment would be forthcoming. The payment, when it arrived, was nothing more than I'd received as a last minute replacement against Albert Carroll and only slightly more than when I'd been back up to Dundee for a rematch with Jimmy Croll. That was my first fight since Italy and after the happiness, warmth and the pay cheque of that particular trip, the Café Royal reminded me of the worst England can be when you are excluded from it, or used by it.

Embraced by the cigar smoke, myself and Santos Martins were led out on to the canvas to polite applause. It was the third time I faced the Nigerian and it was clear that he regarded his chances of glory with much more seriousness than I did. We had drawn the first and I had won the second. Now Martins was out for revenge and he calculated for it. He had thought about what had gone wrong in the previous two fights, he had assessed his own tactical faults and my strengths and he had come up with a strategy to defeat me. I had rarely done that. I was not a boxer who considered the way I fought anymore out of the ring than in it. I trusted in the moment and my own dogmatism and something, rightly or wrongly, called heart. Not that I lacked the will to succeed. In the ring I expended everything I had and I always trained hard, but it was the absence of any knowledge that what I was doing was not enough, not contrived enough, is where I failed.

Without a doubt, this was a result of erratic and untutored preparation, both when training on the booths and as a result of Jack Turner's opinion of his boxers as commercial property rather than trained athletes. The Colonel's intentions were always impeccable, but his expertise was lacking and even though Len had what I needed, we never worked together full-time. Training at the Thomas à Becket I was always envious and full of questions that began 'what if...?' What if I had been born in London? What if I had had Danny Holland or Snowy Buckingham to train me? What if I had had Mickey Duff as my manager? It seemed, in mid-December that the year, which had begun with such disciplined hope on white winter mornings in the New Forest, was ending drowned in cynicism. There would however be another resuscitation of glory and ambition, but first I had to face Santos Martins in the silence of the Café Royal.

We were both hard punchers, but he had worked out that he simply had to be quicker or find a way of effecting that quickness. He assumed the role of authority early in the fight and never relinquished it, not even when I managed to force through a big left hook. Every time I did he wouldn't allow it to open up the fight. He had me down in the second round and I hauled myself up on the count of seven. Of course, there was no winning over the crowd, who would almost certainly be on the side of the white Britain over the black African. The main noises, apart from the soft chatter, were the squeak of our boots on the canvas, the involuntary sounds rising from our bodies and blunt thud of our gloves on each other; the only experience that came half as close was sparring in an empty gym. One spectator had obviously drunk a brandy too many and he let go a reprimand at my obvious inferiority. A forceful voice sounded somewhere from the shadows and called him back to restraint: "Order gentlemen, please!" The points decision was unanimous and Martins won, which I was already resigned to. Then the neat rows stood and applauded more vigorously than before, holding their cigars in their mouths, but still as if they were showing their appreciation of a social experiment rather than a boxing match.

After Italy and before going back up to Dundee, my sister Edna and I had moved from Bournemouth to London. She had made the decision to emigrate to Canada and as she had to wait for all the lengthy paperwork, it seemed more sensible to be in London where all the formalities took place. My training then shifted full-time to the Becket. I had to look after myself to an extent, as the trainers were generally busy concentrating on the other boxers, but the sparring was good. Edna and I were together in London for a month or two and then she left. I moved in with a friend, Peter Jones for a time and then found myself a flat in Battersea. My list of friends in London was short and almost purely boxing based, so when I was reacquainted with the sister of a friend from my days of National Service, I asked her to go out for a drink with me. Her name was Greta and we had always got on very well in each other's company. Absolutely a London girl, she had a smart tongue and electric temper. She was small and alongside my battered hands, hers looked like the most exquisite form of human perfection. She had brown eyes like chestnuts and with the money I earned from the Martins fight I bought her a coat from Swan and Edgar in the West End.

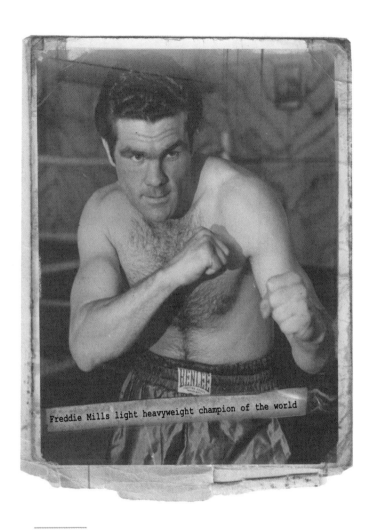

Freddie Mills light heavyweight champion of the world

Freddie Mills

CHAPTER 22

A SAVAGE SYSTEM

Amateurs deal in dreams. Professionals, even champions, deal in hard cash. Sport has always been closer to everyday life than we like to admit. Why throw away a talent for some honourable notion you don't believe in? Would a concert pianist wait tables, or fix refrigerators if he could earn a good living playing for diners at a restaurant? All and every man who has ever boxed for a living understands this.

Freddie Mills understood this when we appeared together on an entertainment programme called 'Saturday Night Out'; a weekly live TV broadcast, presented by Bob Danvers-Walker. Freddie, who topped the bill, was a colourful, courageous fighter, a folk hero loved by the public and media alike. Before he had become the light heavyweight boxing champion of the world in 1948, he had learnt his trade on the boxing booths. The BBC had set up a boxing ring to replicate the feel of the fairground booths and asked real boxers to fill it with real action. After the show, the BBC man asked me how much I wanted for my fee. I was about to say ten quid when Freddie chipped in: "He wants forty quid and travelling expenses." The BBC man gave me fifty. Freddie absolutely understood.

That evening, as Freddie sauntered cheerfully into the night, he had fame, good looks, a fair amount of fortune and a happy family. However, his life was to end in tragic circumstances. In July 1965 he was found dead in the back of his Citroen car parked in Goslett Yard, Soho, behind his nightclub. He was only forty-three and had been shot in the head with a rifle. His family and many of his closest friends, who included celebrities and criminals, were convinced he had been murdered, but the police ruled his death a suicide. There were so many rumours and theories; none of it added up. Chrissie, his widow, believed that local gangsters who had been extorting large amounts of money from club owners had killed him.

The boxing world and the criminal underworld were inextricably linked in those days and wherever there is cash you'll find gangsters. I have always found it amusing when people talk about being able to leave their doors unlocked and how these gangsters were so good to their mums. You are all right with them as long as you've got nothing worth taking. All I know is that Freddie Mills was always good to me in whatever dealings we had; occasionally I used to service the fridges at his club. There was a good documentary made about him some years ago, *The Freddie Mills Story*.

Randolph Turpin also ended up dying of gunshot wounds, in down-at-heel circumstances. He had once promised one of his friends, fairground booth operator Pat McKeown "If I win a world title, I'll pop down and box on your booth." On 10 July 1951 at Earls Court, Turpin stunned the boxing world by beating Sugar Ray Robinson for the middleweight championship of the world. Just three weeks or so later I was performing on a booth at Queen's Park, Aldershot, when a shining Rolls Royce purred up and in the back was the new champion. Turpin had kept his promise and took part in a gee-up fight against a chap called Danny Hagan. Sadly, after eventually losing his title, Turpin's money and friends disappeared. Ten months after Mills' death, Turpin committed suicide after apparently shooting his four-year-old daughter Carmen, in a Leamington Spa flat.

My first fight of 1955 was against Ron Richardson, a relative of the Richardson brothers, who were leaders of the Richardson gang and some time rivals of the Krays. The fight was at Epsom Baths in Surrey and Richardson was a substitute fighter, but on a good run of form. The cameras were there too, not the BBC but Gaumont British newsreels. I hadn't trained as hard for this fight after the lull of Christmas and I wasn't feeling on top form. The fight began slowly with Richardson strictly avoiding me as I went on the attack. Then, whether it was a preconceived tactic, or he was reacting to my sluggishness, he suddenly reared to meet me. His punches started getting through with less inhibition and by the final round I knew it was my fight to pull back. I was getting some good left hooks in, not my strongest but they seemed to be hurting Richardson and then out of nowhere came a short right-handed jab that staggered me. I never won back the initiative. Richardson was declared the winner by the shortest of distances. I had now been beaten five times in succession. This still mattered, even if the ignominy of defeat no longer did. Aside from the emotional upheaval of sport, boxing as a business was still determined for each individual by the victory and loss count. A losing fighter gets paid less. I still needed to win; I was not going to make much money by losing.

With this cold and professional attitude I resolved to prepare for my next fight as I had in the past, in order to avoid slipping into receiving paltry paychecks for what would increasingly become a beating. It is the natural cruelty of boxing that the more physical suffering you endure, the less recompense you get for your trouble. I knew many ageing men who became the victims of such a savage system and their experience had taught me to be ruthless.

Jack Turner was at the periphery of my arrangements by then, but he continued to organise fights in the role of my manager. There was now even less pressure on him to exert himself in lobbying promoters for a progressive fight, or even one that paid well. In February he phoned and said that he had arranged a bout for the beginning of March against Rees Moore. Just ten months earlier he had arranged my second fight against the Welsh champion and for my third time in the ring with Moore I simply accepted it as the fisherman accepts another day of water and nets, or the miner another of heat and coal: without complaint. Perhaps this was to be a barometer of how far my prospects had fallen within a year.

Greta was now a serious girlfriend, and made the trip up to Leicester with me: it was the first time she had come to one of my fights. Almost immediately the opening bell rang, I could hear Greta screaming at me in her uncompromising London accent. I couldn't make out what she was saying but I could hear it all right, even above the noise of the crowd. I tried to concentrate on boxing; I really tried. We fought for an unremarkable two minutes and then I had to react. I held my gloves up at Moore, who stopped, perplexed. Everyone had stopped, wondering at my extraordinary behavior, even the referee. Perhaps this is what John Graham Chambers had in mind when he wrote, 'Should the contest be stopped by any unavoidable interference'. I walked over to the rope just above where the now silent Greta was seated. My words were something along the lines of "I'm trying to have a bloody fight in this ring so sit down and shut up!" The crowd roared with laughter, even Moore, and we touched gloves and went back at it. Greta, of course, didn't appreciate it as much as everyone else, but that was the post-fight fight and until then I could at least concentrate on Moore.

I was determined not to make this a sixth loss. My record against Moore, two wins and a draw, gave me confidence but also added pressure. I knew that I had to breach him early if I was not to be frustrated by his continual retreat. To this end I attacked him mercilessly and by the fifth he was wavering. A firm body shot had him down on the canvas and after that he didn't want to know. The point's decision was emphatic; one of the largest I ever had. This stopped the decline and for that I was more relieved then triumphant.

A perfect example of boxers becoming victims of the system that only rewards the victor, was Kurt Ernst. He was the supreme youthful stylist when we were learning at the Apollo and we were together on the same bill many times throughout our professional careers. Kurt was there as a substitute that night in Leicester. Gordon Goodman had been hit by flu and pulled out of his fight against Darky Hughes, and Kurt had obliged a late 200-mile trip to stand in. Unfortunately the 200 miles wasn't the worst of it for Kurt that night, he got badly beaten by Hughes, his left eye closed and an unabating flow of blood streamed from his nose. I didn't dare ask how much he received for such an evening.

My next fight was the desire of my opponent for revenge. Almost two years previously I had humiliated this boxer at Wembley Town Hall by knocking him out in under a minute. It seemed that all this time he had been quietly scheming and holding a grudge, wanting to repay me for that night. Perhaps he had noticed my decline in form and sensed his opportunity. According to Jack, his manager had asked for a rematch before we were even out of the changing rooms. It was unlike Jack to refuse for so long, or more likely that he had been persuaded to let the grudge rest for a while. However, by the end of March 1956, Leo Maloney had his long awaited chance.

The venue was Great Yarmouth Hippodrome and the promoter, Cliff Butler, trumpeted what he called my 'sensational win' over Boswell St Lewis a year earlier. I had a mixed history with the Hippodrome; I lost there to Roy Baird and then had the ecstatic win against St Lewis. The return fight against Leo Maloney further complicated my feelings towards the venue. Not because of the fight itself, but because of the Norfolk crowd, who were firmly Maloney's side. Due to my uncompromising style I was used to getting a favourable crowd reaction, even in London against a Londoner. So being heckled and booed was an unsettling experience for me.

I opened the fight with my usual barrage and Maloney weathered it well. I could sense that he really didn't want to lose as he was cagey and didn't give much light between his defense. He struck out with rapid counters, which can be devastating if done skillfully. It was obvious that he had come to the fight well versed in the tactic. Still, I was managing to dictate the fight; it is almost inevitable when fighting against such a technique, unless you become completely undisciplined and are made desperate by the frustration.

By the end of the fight I had certainly been the more aggressive. Maloney had boxed well but he had not managed to dominate me. For this I felt I was worth the win and the judges agreed. As the referee raised my hand the crowd made their displeasure known with boos and catcalls. This nasty experience, of being the subject of so much ill feeling, was unique to me and caused a strange sense of powerlessness. I was confident that I had deserved the win, but I just couldn't fathom the crowd.

Despite this Jack organised my next fight, less than a month later, at the same venue. This time against Albert Carroll who had already beaten me on points. It was a non-starter of a fight, neither of us making any sort of headway, until in the sixth round an innocuous punch cut me above my eye and it bled badly enough for the referee to call it a technical knockout. But that wasn't the end of my ignominy. In the fifties you sometimes found yourself on a bus with the rest of the bill, winners and losers all cramped in for the return journey. This was how it had been arranged for the Albert Carroll fight. Sat on the bus, surrounded by boxers and their entourages, my cut just wouldn't stop bleeding. I was despairing of ever damming the flow until Harry Gibbs, the legendary referee, quietly leant over and handed me his perfectly clean white handkerchief, telling me quietly to keep it.

Then came the fight that convinced me I had to give up. It was at Harringay Arena, a huge white fin of a building. The atmosphere that night was of muttering aggravation and annoyance, made claustrophobic by the June heat. One of those summer nights when the world seems messy and fugitive. Top of the bill at Harringay was the World Light-Heavyweight Title fight with Archie Moore, the Old Mongoose, defending against Yolande Pompey. I was against Tony Barrett, a tall lorry driver from Pimlico who was stabled with Jack Solomon. After us Peter Waterman would continue his rise by claiming the British Welterweight Title from Wally Thoms. I didn't see the Waterman-Thoms fight, I only read about it the next day. But I did see Archie Moore's mastery as we were scheduled to appear immediately after him and Pompey.

Moore was unbelievably comfortable. He always looked the strongest, the most firm on his feet, but this doesn't always signify a victory in boxing. However, with Moore there was never any doubt. Pompey took a couple of counts on one knee in the final round, with Moore looking as fresh as if he had just jumped off the stool for the first time. For the ending, which seemed abrupt, Moore forced Pompey into the corner immediately after the second count and the referee intervened as Pompey's arms, raised in defence, began to shake alarmingly as they were breached three times. Moore retained the title. I sparred with Pompey at the Becket, I wouldn't have liked to do the same with Moore.

Moore boxed into his forties, long before it became unusual to do so, and he starred in films. Pompey married a prostitute in Victoria. Somehow he lost all his earnings from boxing and he languished in poverty. I knew this because I once bumped into him on Chelsea Bridge in London and we had a drink together in a nearby pub. After hearing his situation I gave him a fiver out of sentiment for the fraternity of boxers. I never saw him again.

As for my fight against Barrett, I knew he could box but I didn't think he could punch. We reached the end of the sixth round. In the previous three I had felt in control and knew I would win if it went to points. Barratt's lack of a strong punch didn't herald his ability to get a knockout, so I was feeling confident as I sat on my

189

JACK SOLOMONS presents the

Lightheavyweight Championship OF THE World

HARRINGAY ARENA

TUESDAY 5th JUNE 1956

ARCHIE MOORE v YOLANDE POMPEY

CHAMPION   CONTENDER

OFFICIAL PROGRAMME 2'-

stool ready for the seventh. What came next was absolutely unexpected and unique in my career. Midway through the round he threw an unanticipated right and I stepped straight into it. I must have been out before I hit the floor. I didn't feel a thing until I woke up in the changing room with Jack Turner and Jack Solomons standing over me. Solomons was repeatedly asking me who he was, and pointing to Turner with the same question. It took a while before I gathered my senses and could reply. Solomons looked almost paternally at me and said that tomorrow I was going to see Dr Caplin in Harley Street.

It was the only knockout of my career. I remember Freddie Mills once said that you're not a boxer until you've been knocked out. After it happened to me, I wasn't so sure about Freddie's wisdom. Dr Caplin said that there would be no lasting damage but that I should leave it at least six weeks before I boxed again. I replied that I intended to leave it at least six months, and that was that. I left the sport quietly and indefinitely. Right then I had no plans in which boxing featured.

PART FOUR

FINAL
ROUNDS

ANOTHER KIND OF RING
A COMEBACK
OUT-BOXED
MICKEY DUFF
THE FINAL BELL

CHAPTER 23

ANOTHER KIND OF RING

At first I didn't miss it at all. Boxing was no longer the persistent concern it had been and my desire to get in the ring had lost its urgency. So I turned towards other things and a different kind of ring. My impending marriage to Greta, our relationship, enveloped us both as new love always does and we got married at St Saviour's Church in Battersea. Len was there with his wife Blossom, and the Colonel and Eric made the trip from Scotland. It was the first time I had seen them in a year. I remember the sweet scent of whisky on the air and the Colonel commenting on how much he thought I had changed. This surprised me. I felt it might have been a reflection of his own concerns as he had aged visibly. I introduced him to Greta, he was his well-bred charming self and he delighted her. But that was our last ever meeting. His time in my life had been like a golden afternoon, so close to hope and fulfilment. But now there was nothing I could do to regain that feeling. My decision to put boxing on hold was the culmination of the steadily mounting anti-feeling that had begun in the wake of the Colonel's exit and the Waterman fight. Wishing him farewell after the wedding, I didn't know that it would be our final goodbye, but in retrospect it seems appropriate that it happened then. Contentment followed, as brief as the morning. Greta and I honeymooned a week in north Devon, in an ancient pub called The Hoops Inn. Then we spent a week in Torquay with my mother and I showed my new wife the sights and my old haunts.

Work began soon after we returned to London, true grinding work, the nature of which I wasn't used to. My new father-in-law suggested that I try steel fixing, as he had contacts in the business who would be glad to give me work on his recommendation. He said that working in the open air would be good for an active lad like me. It was not easy. In the heat, when the sun shone, the metal would get hot and burn my hands. In the cold, when water froze, it would bond my hands to the steel. I couldn't wear gloves for protection, as the steel would slip from my grasp. The wage was prompt and regular, but it was paltry when compared to what I could earn boxing.

I would still run to stay reasonably fit, but I didn't attend a gym. Occasionally I would find myself short of money and dwell on how lucrative it was in the ring, and how much I had let slip through my fingers. I would get invitations to watch fights and sometimes I accepted. Then, in the familiar arena, the sounds of the crowd hurling faithless emotion and the announcer intoning the boxer's names, would bring that surging adrenaline feeling and I would just stand and absorb myself into the mass of desperate, baying spectators. But by the end, when I had seen four or five boxers wilt and fold, every vestige of power drained from their limbs, I quickly retreated from the thrill of pugilism and remembered why I had stopped.

Sometime after our wedding, the vicar who had married us called round to our house and asked if I would help in setting up a boxing section for his youth club that he had ironically named Old Campaigners. He said that no one else he knew had the knowledge to get the boxing lessons started and that the kids had stolen half the equipment. I wasn't overly enthusiastic but I agreed because it was difficult to say no to a priest and because Greta leaned on me. As an opening gambit, to win their respect and in an attempt to establish order, I asked if they would like to meet boxers like Terry Spinks, who had just won gold at the Melbourne Olympics. They weren't shy in making it known that they would and so I told them they had first to return all the missing equipment. It worked. Everything came back the next week apart from a pair of gloves that one boy admitted he had already sold. They never did get Terry Spinks, but they forgot about him and in the end didn't need him. They all took to boxing and as an added extra we would all go across to Clapham Common to play football.

This makeshift gym, which reminded me of my first boxing school in Torquay, Snip Cornish's YMCA dojo, was the reason I started back on the road to the professional game. No matter that these were kids who had never fought anything other than with their siblings and in streets fights. Their naivety and delight at learning how to control their arms, how to block and how to position their feet until they could spar with each other and develop their own insignificant rivalries, was my first taste of something I would take on after I had finished with boxing for good. But for now it served to remind me of my own romance with the sport. At least the Old Campaigners gave me back the spirit, the mysterious compulsion to box, but there was also a more hard-headed and practical reason. Money.

Every week, as I collected my wages, it would hit me that I could be earning so much more than this. That I had wasted so much more than this. That I had boxed professionally for more than four years and only had scars and friends to show for it. Scars and friends could be had in plenty of jobs, but not the money you could get from boxing. Belts, titles, they were old dreams by now. They were indeed something to be had from boxing along with the accompanying adulation, celebrity and reverence. But I was just one of those obscure, middling fighters who held up the whole business and who, if they weren't careful, would get used by the business. I wanted my portion and I wanted it in figures. But it wasn't only this. I had seen, touched and experienced the tedious industrial fight to survive. I knew I was lucky enough to have a way out, if not forever, then for a while at least.

Jack Turner was still my manager but our five-year contract was almost up. During my period out of the ring he occasionally rang me with offers of fights. As ruthlessly money minded as he had always been, I knew he would continue to match me with anyone who came along. Not that my opponents' boxing renown really mattered anymore, but there is a correlation between skill and payment. I was the one getting hit, so I didn't want just any money. In the event, I visited the Becket and got talking to Nobby Wallace, who told me that Jack King, matchmaker at the National Sporting Club, was looking for good fighters. Of course I knew King from the Café Royal and so telephoned him to offer my services. I did this well in advance of any actual appearance in the ring. After six months of only roadwork and training kids, I was far from fit. My muscles had atrophied somewhat and I doubted if my prized left hook had retained much of its former power. Nevertheless, the informal arrangement with Jack King served as something to work towards.

At the start, even the Becket was out of the question. Peter Jones suggested I try an amateur club and he put me in touch with the Caius. Amateur boxing was something I could handle straight away, the skill and fitness levels being so much lower than in the professional ranks. I spent about a month there before I felt confident and sharp enough to approach Danny Holland and Nobby Wallace at the Becket. It was quite a shock. It was as if I had forgotten the level at which I used to box, and how honed and demanding professionalism could be. My first week consisted of painful punches and painful lungs, but I needed to experience that level and be up against it again in order to regain the standard. Gradually I began to feel good again. The re-germination of the fighting seed grew in my body and mind. As a result I became fresher and stronger than I had felt in all of the long bitter year before I gave up.

CHAPTER 24

A COMEBACK

I had been in the top ten welterweight division before I had taken my sabbatical and there was no way I could expect it afterwards. The memory of my ability had lingered just enough to earn me a place in the four star section; a group of fighters ranked below the elite who boxed each other, the consistent winners gaining the chance to take on one of the fighters from the top ten. Generally top ten fighters fought against each other but there was no rule to this and it was not unusual for a four star boxer to fight a top ten boxer; in fact it was imperative for the progression of the sport. It was up to individual managers to square bouts through the promoters. I was rarely involved with this side of boxing and its complexities failed me.

In the four star section there was a mixture of green youth and veterans. I was a veteran if only for my cynicism. In 1957 Peter Waterman was champion, Tommy Molloy was his closest challenger and his brother Leo, who I had beaten twice, was ranked fourth. In the four star section there was the likes of Roy Baird, Ron Richardson and Syd Greb. Baird and Richardson had both beaten me before. Greb was a hard Liverpudlian with a useful left and it was his name that Jack King mentioned when he rang me up with an opportunity to return to the Café Royal. Jack Turner had nothing at all to do with this. Our contract had not lawfully expired but I felt sufficiently on the edge of it and out of Jack's consciousness to act for myself. The platform of the National Sporting Club gave me that opportunity.

It wasn't a difficult decision but I only had two weeks to spirit myself up to some kind of peak performance again. All my training during the previous months had achieved a springing level of fitness but sharpness in the ring can only be tested in the ring. Greb had begun as a lightweight and so was moving up a division to match my weight. It wasn't the first time he had done it, but I had my suspicions that he might have some trouble, thus giving me an advantage. There was no doubt that this was my test of re-admittance. Jack King made clear his unsentimental attitude. "Chuck him in. If he loses, chuck him out again." Of course Jack King wasn't the only promoter, but everyone who mattered would take notice of the results. It was almost as if King was speaking for the whole of boxing's power structure.

I had been developing a new style for my comeback, after reasoning that I might have lost some of my explosive power and tenacity during my lay off. My plan was to be what had always frustrated me, a boxer who tries to avoid being hit. I had decided to dispense with the wild hooks that served me so well in the past as they were too high a risk. Counter-attack was to be tight and controlled. It was in this pattern I tried to train. Danny Holland responded to my wishes at the Becket and tried to coax a new fighter out of me despite his obvious scepticism.

My strategy of avoiding getting hit took its first blow in the first minute of the first fight. Not only was I on the end of a punch, I found myself down on the canvas inhaling its familiar scent. I managed not to panic, taking the majority of the count and regaining my feet as if nothing had happened. It was fortunate that this harsh lesson happened at the beginning when I was fresh enough to learn from it – that I was the same fighter who had left the ring nine months previously, only slower. Despite this, I carried on with my plan of avoiding Greb's punches, because I needed to feel comfortable again in the ring and because I thought that it was a winning formula. He kept piling in and flashed through my defences to graze my chin with a swift right. But that was his only shot of any significance. By the fourth, my memory had been stimulated enough and that is when I began to have my say. I attacked his body relentlessly and made him retrace his steps across the canvas. Then the crowd began to feel the fire of the fight and warmed appropriately, clapping restrainedly and tinkling their shots on the rocks a little more excitedly. Greb's left hand, as adept at defence as attack, was difficult to pass, but by the end I was back and scrapping like a voracious animal. If the first half was Greb's then the second was mine. If a round of clapping can be described as an explosion then that is what happened, the crowd's appreciation was evident. A small seed of optimism lay in the back of my mind and ventured the thought that I could be granted a victory for my efforts. Not quite, it was a draw. However, that seemed fair and not a failure.

What actually helped me pass Jack King's test was, I think, an article in the *Boxing News* and King's own lack of imagination. The article appeared the day after the fight and lauded mine and Greb's fight as an unusually exciting spectacle for the Café Royal. It then went on to find fault with the rule of silence that forbade the forming of an atmosphere, commenting that the fight should have been awarded to Greb, rather than as a draw. I knew the scrutiny with which promoters and managers read the press and the influence it had on them. By stating 'Paul King and Syd Greb was the only bout worth taking notes on', the article had done more than enough for Jack King to think of me as a good draw. Not only this but the nobbins split between the two of us were almost enough to double our wages for the night. This expression of approval from the crowd was enough to make their forced silence irrelevant.

From this evidence Jack King knew he needed more fights like this one and so under a month later, we were back for a rematch, with King hoping for a repeat of the first bout. After the rewards of the last fight I was only too pleased to take Greb on again, this time with the extra confidence of knowing the expectations and a feeling that I could fulfil them. King got what he wanted almost too well, another thriller that was tempered yet again by the indecision of the judges. I felt certain I had performed better than in the first fight. Several journalists agreed with me, whilst taking the opportunity to fault the National Sporting Club for its inability to attain a standard in the running of its boxing matches, which was a favourite pastime of the British boxing press in the mid-fifties. For myself I had proved that I could still hold my own and reap financial rewards. It had been sixteen full rounds and I had boxed to a standard successful enough to carry out the plan for the continuation of my boxing career.

After the two draws with Greb (who reminded me of a tough little bastard from my early career, Johnny Fish), my fights became dominated by two names: Richardson and Molloy. I subsequently found myself trapped in a labyrinth of rematches and slowly dissipating hopes. The first of eight final fights was against Ron Richardson, a second encounter after losing to him in early 1956. Again the fight was held in the repressed rooms of the Café Royal. My brother-in-law Harold was a keen boxing fan, our mutual interest in the sport had been a bond during National Service. He had seen Richardson box several times and gave me a piece of valuable advice: use mainly my left hand and jab like mad. He knew that keeping Richardson at arm's length was the best policy, he had seen Albert Carroll do it at Clapham Greyhound Track and win a points victory. In the absence of any real training team or guidance, I was now improvising. Harold's opinion was the best I had.

In the past I was always the one to get frustrated. With Harold's advice well carried out, Richardson boiled. I could see his face writhing at his inability to close the distance between us as I jabbed back at each of his forays. It took enormous concentration to keep it up and there were moments when I felt the whole thing would collapse and I would be left helpless, stuck in a groove not knowing how to get out. But apart from a heavy blow to the temple that had me taking a count, I kept up my plan, staved him off and kept breaking through at his face, forcing him to retreat, piling up the points. I impressed myself with my own discipline and clearness of mind to carry out an almost ad hoc plan through eight rounds of boxing. The bout was recorded by Gaumont British News and highlights were broadcast. Len phoned to congratulate me on the manner of my victory, which was a near perfect demonstration of the new style I had tried to implement for my comeback and the only time it was successful. It was belatedly the kind of boxing Len had always hoped from me. In the end my victory was confirmed by an emphatic margin on points. So for my comeback I had two draws and a victory, an unbeaten run.

This run continued into the next fight too. I was to box Leo Molloy from Birkenhead, an excellent lightweight. After fighting the odd welterweight bout, three fights previous to our encounter, Molloy had moved up a division permanently. He was also on a three game unbeaten streak and had just drawn with my old opponent the Scot, Jimmy Croll. Molloy was a local boy at The Stadium in Liverpool, which was where he was fighting most of his bouts at that time. The Stadium was an extraordinary venue, an umbilical cord of fighting tradition on Merseyside. The Liverpudlians were full of fervour for boxing, and although they always supported their own, they did not make me feel like a villain simply because of my presence. I have excellent memories of fighting in Liverpool.

I began the fight well and floored Molloy in round two, a right cross onto the nose which he certainly hadn't seen coming. The blow visibly unbalanced him and it took some effort for him to get up. Even when he did, I forced him onto the ropes and he could not properly defend himself. The bell sounded at the critical moment for him. There was more favourable reaction from the crowd when I put him down a second time in the next round. I was switching my attack from head to body very precisely and it was a firm hit to his side that did for him again. But he was from seafaring, urban toughness and could withstand it. He fought back and regained his standing. His own right cross cut my nose. He hit me several times in the same place above the left eye and caused it to split open. With the sight of blood the crowd anticipated victory and screamed louder in support of Molloy.

There was no doubt I had been in the lead during the early rounds but Molloy managed to diminish the gap later on in the fight. There was a desperate flurry when at the tipping point of either victory or defeat we each tried to influence the seesaw in our favour. The last rounds were frenetic and I had the feeling of elation that sport offers from a breathless contest, despite the result. The decision was unpredictable. It was a draw again. In four fights I had doubled my career total.

CHAPTER 25

OUT-BOXED

A boxer with any kind of aspirations needs to be at the gym. At this point in my career I had double the reasons to be there on a regular basis. Of course I had to keep up my physical condition, but having no manager meant that I relied on the dissolute promoters who made cautious phone calls to gyms in order to pad out their bill of fighters. Having a reputation of sorts made me, for a short time, a prize for such businessmen, who didn't expect any pedigree from fighters, even when phoning a gym like the Becket. Attending the gym fulfilled both my practical and business obligations. Danny Holland or Nobby Wallace would take the phone, listen to the man on the other end, hear who he already had fighting and pick the boxer most suitable to match him. This was how I had got the Molloy fight in Liverpool.

It was the first venture as a promoter for the former Arsenal forward Ralph Birkett. He was a deep west-country boy and he held his first night of boxing at Torquay town hall. It had been two years since I had been in a local ring, my last fight in Torquay I had beaten Santos Martins, immediately after the Peter Waterman fight. When Birkett phoned the Becket, saying he needed a welterweight to fight Ron Richardson, Danny Holland immediately thought of me. Danny said I was the only one suitable and told him that Richardson and I had already fought twice and Richardson had been on the receiving end. Birkett apparently said I would be perfect. In my mind, I was ready to reject the bout straight off, but before I spoke out loud, I remembered why I was in boxing and that a fight against a man I had just beaten, but who was ranked highly, was the perfect opportunity for a good night's earning. So I accepted.

When formulating my plan for a comeback I had not counted on the influence other aspects of life can have on boxing. When, in the build-up to the third Richardson fight, I found out that I was going to be a father, the news caused some disruption. The celebrations of the pregnancy and the attention Greta demanded, meant that I often missed my training sessions and gained several pounds that had to be shed. I trained when I could, which was not often enough for an impending fight. Most of my poor performances were a result of leaving it too late to burn off weight.

Unfortunately for me, Ron Richardson was extremely fit and in tip top condition, the best I had ever seen him. It was one of those fights where you feel beaten from the outset and you stay feeling beaten until the referee has confirmed it at the end. In the second round, an unimpeded left hook almost ripped my lower jaw from my skull and from then on I felt even more forlornly lost than I had in the previous round. I discarded my strategy that had tangled Richardson in anger and helplessness in our previous fight and I returned atavistically to a blind rescue. I hooked wildly in an effort to tame him and force my way desperately back into the fight, but each attempt was doomed. That I was upright to hold the referees hand after the final moments I consider more luck than design, in the seventh Richardson opened the full force of his punching barrage and I bore the brunt of every blow. By that time I knew I had lost everything. I continued to fight back, catching him several times between the moments in which he wasn't attacking. But perhaps by that time he felt he could afford to absorb punches masochistically in the knowledge that his supremacy had been fixed.

That night there was also a final appearance for Kurt Ernst in the narrative of my boxing career. On that warm July evening in Torquay we crossed the same ring for the last time. He seemed the perennial substitute and there cannot have been a situation more indicative of the business of boxing in the fifties than the one that led Kurt Ernst to be fighting in Torquay that evening. The fight programme and poster had the bout as Teddy Barker against Terry Mohale but Mohale had injured his arm on the day of the fight. So uncompromising were the organisers that Jim Alden, the Western Area secretary for the Boxing Board of Control, took a taxi to Kurt's house to seek him out personally for the fight that day. Alden found him dressed up and ready to take Mrs Ernst to the cinema. A short time and a brief chat later Kurt had abandoned his seat in the stalls for a stool in the ring. Fighting before me that night, he came good and won handsomely on points. Kurt Ernst: a youthful prodigy, a torridly professional boxer, eclipsed and lapsing through my days in the ring. He fought his last fight only a month after my own.

Either Danny or Nobby, I can't remember which, told me of that there was a fight happening in Southampton. Albert Carroll was lined up as the opponent; he had beaten me twice, but that didn't put me off. The pay was a sustantial sixty pounds and the consequences of losing were minimal, far outstripped by the consequences of winning, which would certainly go some way to re-establishing my status in the upper echelons of the welter-weight division. I still had memories of the fight in Streatham when I had floored him with a monumental punch, only to be astonished as he raised himself up before the count was out. His other victory over me had been a technical knockout, merely a gushing cut that would not be staunched. This time I thought I could win.

However, it did not turn out how I wished. It was the first fight in which I felt my ability to box weakening. Despite my two previous losses to Carroll there was no real gap between our abilities and yet I found myself out-boxed. I continually walked into his right-hand as I tried to attack. Walking into your opponents' punches opens up your defence like nothing else. Carroll would go as far as losing a British Welterweight Title bout. He was an excellent boxer but I felt myself beginning to wane. Carroll won on points. I took home sixty pounds.

Paul King and Leo Molloy

CHAPTER 26

MICKEY DUFF

Then came Mickey Duff. Of course I knew him, but I didn't know enough. It was only later that I realised the full extent of his power. Danny Holland was away with Henry Cooper, so it was Nobby Wallace who acted as intermediary. Perhaps because trainers earn a regular wage and are concerned with the technicalities of boxing, and managers are concerned with the money they can get out of the sport, fighters tend to trust the opinion of their trainers more. The camaraderie of the gym is binding. So when Nobby gave his opinion that Mickey Duff would be good for my career, or what was left of it, I was prepared to consider it.

Mickey Duff talked more than anyone I had ever met. People have often said the same thing about me, but I found myself over-whelmed by Mickey. However, what he had to say certainly didn't lack quality. Nevertheless, in my mind, I kicked against it. I had my own personal plan, which had been so cynical and unambitious that it had been working. Then Duff unknowingly hijacked it by spinning off figures that surpassed what I earned from many of my more prestigious bouts. As an opening he was offering me a rematch with Leo Molloy, who I had drawn with the previous May. And it was to be at the same wild venue, The Stadium in Liverpool. The bout, the purse, I knew I couldn't get either of these through the telephonic whisperings of desperate promoters to Nobby and Danny. But that wasn't all. Duff had larger and longer plans and he appealed to my sentiment by assuring me that if I regained my earlier form he would make sure I got a title shot.

It had been two years since I had entertained thoughts of success on this scale, that was back when I was with the Colonel and had

Len Harvey in my corner. Even though my idea of Duff's power was a huge underestimation, I believed that he could engineer a title bout for the right boxer. Being the right boxer, however, was something I would have to live up to. So I convinced myself that I could be that boxer and invented excuses for my bad form and my slide down the rankings. I told myself that it was merely my desire, my will that was lacking; my talent was still there. All I had to do was want it enough and I would once again be on the road to becoming a champion.

I don't think I was entirely to blame for this illusion. Mickey Duff's smooth salesmanship was also responsible, though with hindsight it is hard to tell if he ever actually believed as I did. It speaks a lot that Mickey Duff thought my ability and my early record impressive enough to be worthy of a title challenge. I often thought that if I had not had Jack as my manager, if I had first been spotted by someone shrewder and less myopic, if I had been with someone like Mickey Duff from the start, then perhaps everything would have different. But the fates, the gods, blind chance, only gave him to me when all was lost.

However, now I had Mickey Duff and he offered a good deal of money and a chance to reach the top again. My travel to Liverpool had beem arranged for me; a train north and a sleeper south, no long, uncomfortable journeys. If nothing else, this impressed me straight away. It was a way of doing things that had been absent since the Colonel and Eric had taken care of my affairs. The Stadium was the closest to perfect of all the boxing venues I ever fought at. I remember how the crowd's energy seemed a chaotic tide of noise crashing in waves against the ring, over and over. The only way through the vibrations was concentration, total mental commitment to the action. It felt significant to be stood in the ring that evening and with all that had been invested in me, I felt confident.

I came out like a sprinter and bounded for the lead immediately.

I caught him twice, in quick succession, forcing my way through his defence. But in doing so I was too cavalier and he struck back mightily, knocking me down with a vicious left hook, releasing a tidal wave of noise from the crowd. Yet I was not overawed. In the second round I gave him back what he had given me and met him at eye-level with my laces after a right cross had struck his cheek. The crowd screeched and clamoured in brutal ecstasy. The middle of the fight broke out into a series of rapid punching rallies where one of us would try to increase the pace and the other match it. For the final six minutes I felt myself on top, certainly the stronger fighter, although Molloy did not seem near to weakening. He had a quick, drilling left hand that was impossible to tame and that contrasted to my own heavy punching left hook. Molloy was a good craftsman and by this I mean he could execute, with precision, boxing techniques that can be considered a method, a proven route to success. And yet despite these differences, the officials could not separate us. As I waited for the result to be announced I could not give myself an answer as to whether I had won or not and there was no way Molloy could either. For the histrionic crowd their love of extremities had not been satiated and all the excitement they had witnessed had resulted in a draw. The *Boxing News* spoke for them when it said, 'Another meeting cannot be long delayed and Mersey fans are fervently hoping that does not go to another venue.'

Duff was keen for me to hit some kind of form and he wanted it before the end of the year. So seven days later, before November was out, I was back in the ring. Duff seemed to have devised a method of getting me to prove myself against fighters I had already boxed, first Leo Molloy, now Ron Richardson. Richardson I had beaten but lost to twice. He was a leading contender for the Southern Area Title by that time, so a victory would go some way towards re-establishing my credentials. Looking back I can see how deliberate Duff's moves were and how calculatingly, and with purpose, he managed his boxers.

I turned up at East India Hall in Poplar, East London with a couple of mates, who were chancing it on my arm. The doorman, dour and inflexible, refused them entry. I gave him an ultimatum of all of us or no fight. When pushed, he wasn't as rigid as he appeared and they both bounced in after me, victorious. It was however, the only victory of the night for me. The Molloy fight had been a test. I had summoned all my worth and a bout like that takes more than a week to be rid of. I was tired and working on almost spent reserves. Despite this I managed to take Richardson the distance. The result was no mystery, I knew I had lost. Then there was the unwanted formality of having your wrist gripped by the referee as he raised the other man's arm and the congratulations to Richardson for the third and final time.

However, Mickey Duff wasn't about to give up after two fights. He continued with his push to re-establish me and lined up a mid-December return to The Stadium in Liverpool. Again it was against Molloy, but on this occasion Tommy Molloy. At the time Tommy held the country's longest unbeaten record: twenty-nine fights. In the following year he would win the welterweight title of Great Britain, beating Jimmy Newman on points after fifteen rounds. He would defend it once successfully against Albert Carroll before losing it to Wally Swift. There are always those who are in decline and those on the rise in boxing, half of the fights that came after my break were against future champions or challengers, more if you count those boxed immediately before. But this time Mickey Duff thought I could be the man to inflict a first defeat on Tommy Molloy, or perhaps he was just testing me, asking me to surprise him.

Another sign of Duff's ability was the media speculation and hype in the build-up. There had been virtually none when I had been picking up fights through chance phone calls to the Becket, now there was punditry in the papers and talk on the local radio. They marvelled at Molloy's record, there was no doubt he was the favourite and regarded me as an unpredictable opponent. They had seen in the past what I could do and wondered if I could achieve the unlikely.

In the beginning Molloy didn't display his class. I stalked him, determined to get in first. I wanted to disrupt his strategy, halt any rhythm he might develop and unbalance his certainties. Perhaps this worked, as he appeared ragged. He illustrated his position with a pair of blows that were too low and came from nervous accident rather than foul intention. I must have been ahead on points for most of the fight, Molloy doing just enough to keep himself in it. Then in the sixth I hit him with a left-right combination and he stuttered backwards into a corner, draping himself over the ropes for support. His home crowd showed their excitement at the drama. The final result mattered less to them than the way it was brought about.

Late as it was in the fight, it proved to be my pinnacle. Molloy suddenly and inexplicably found his confidence and mastery. He moved studiously on his feet. He jabbed out rapidly and accurately with his left, finding his way through. My hooks, which had been hurting him, began to become too predictable, too slow. I felt my advantage dwindle and with it my superiority. Something catastrophic had snapped within me and Molloy pushed me around the ring. I was impotent, helpless to do anything but stay on the defensive. The final two rounds couldn't have been more of a contrast to what had gone before and they were decisive. The decision went to Molloy. Thirty unbeaten.

The post-fight period, stretching out over Christmas and New Year, was bleak. My record since my break stood at ten fights: four draws, five losses and a solitary win. Yet somehow the approximations of the ranking system had me as the tenth best welterweight fighter in the country. I still felt as if I could match myself with the best, but the evidence made such confidence seem delusional. However, Mickey Duff gave no signs that his faith was waning. Maybe it was his own ability to reignite my career that he didn't question and maybe he was right. The force of Mickey Duff in the making of champions was unmatched. That winter Duff's extraordinary success was ahead of him and all I could see was Tommy Molloy's left fist coming at my face, again and again.

Even if I had gone on losing, I could still pull in sixty pounds per fight, which meant that if I only boxed once a month I would still be making double what most people earned. My plan on returning had only ever been about money and through prudence I had already saved a significant amount. Mickey Duff had returned me to thoughts of sporting greatness and the losses in the face of this stung me more than they should have. I knew I couldn't subject myself for much longer.

CHAPTER 27

FINAL ROUNDS

After our two breathless draws, the match-up between Leo Molloy and myself was considered to be an exciting prospect. Both our previous fights had gathered a good deal of attention and the boxing media was ready to be entertained again. Even those against the violence of boxing had been drawn in, finding that their souls were sordid enough not to look away. Myself and Molloy could have corrupted Ghandi.

And yet I suffered under my own dark cloud during the build-up. How can you not question your ability when you haven't won for ten fights? Not only this but my weight had ballooned, I was far too heavy to fight a welterweight bout. The only option was the hardest training you could imagine, training where nothing is guaranteed until you have stepped on the scales. However, this time the fat wouldn't shift. January of 1958 was filled with torturous days of physical exertion when I pushed myself to the precipice of my endurance only to find that my weight hadn't altered. I could handle the fights, at just over half an hour and generally weeks apart, but when combined with the training, which had become such a misery for me, the financial rewards and the suspect dreams of boxing glory had become far too little compensation.

I made my decision in the run-up to the fight and I was certain enough to give it voice, though not to Mickey Duff. When I told Danny Holland and Nobby Wallace, their immediate reaction was perplexed, telling me I was crazy, that I had put too much into it and would lose too much. But their arguments came from never having been in a boxing ring. All they could see were the pay cheques and the new manager. They simply didn't understand.

The first two bouts between myself and Leo Molloy had been fought out under the intensity of the mob in Liverpool. For the conclusion of our pugilistic rivalry we were at the Manchester Free Trade Hall, which was a disappointment. The sense of occasion was intensified by having two old friends coming along to watch, Jimmy Malborne and from my army PTI days, Ian George. It was accident rather than design that they were present at what was to be my final bout as they were both unaware of my intentions. Mickey was absent that night, he was with another boxer who had a chance of an area title. It was understandable, but in a way it compounded my feelings that this should be my last fight.

The dark cloud I had been working under broke just before the fight and stormed a tempest over my head; it was not a fitting ending. The first decent punch that Molloy threw I was down. My will to win, my will to box had completely dissipated. I lasted to the sixth. Molloy didn't knock me down again, I threw up my defences for the last time and had enough heart and desire to attempt a few ragged shots. I found the pace difficult to keep up with, not because it was beyond me to do so, but because it was such an effort and that effort now seemed absurd. I knew my time was up, that it was gone forever and that I didn't need to extend it a moment longer. Both my eyes were cut and bleeding and there was only the prospect of more punishment.

At the end of the sixth I returned to my corner and tried to call the referee over. It was someone from Mickey Duff's camp in my corner that night, I had no history with him and I can't even remember his name. Usually the trainers wave their arms at the referee, telling him a fight is over. If it happens between rounds, generally the boxer is in no state to communicate with the referee directly. In this fight I thought only of myself and it didn't even

occur to me to pass my message through Mickey's man. The referee came over, bent down and I told him. It was the end; a technical knockout after six rounds. Leo Molloy came over and hugged me in fraternity.

I stayed in Manchester that night and went drinking with Jimmy Malborne and some others and what with Jimmy's ability to distract and entertain, I found it hard to think that I had just boxed my last professional bout and I got completely drunk. The next day I went back to London, hung-over and sentimental. The same evening I went to the Becket to meet Mickey Duff and tell him simply and straightforwardly that it was all over. He was calm and understanding, we chatted for a while and I handed over his commission from the previous night's fight. I thought he might let me keep it, being my last fight, but he took it from me like a thrifty shop-owner. For him it was simply business. As I left he shook my hand, wished me all the best and said that he wished he'd handled me earlier. So did I. On the walk up the Albany Road, away from the Becket (the first time I had taken that familiar walk without my kitbag), I couldn't help it and I found myself in tears.

For a while it was all too raw to reminisce and I wanted to hear of anything but boxing. Everything seemed to have ended in disappointment and I wished so many things could have been different. And then over time, I began to be proud of what I had achieved. Going no further seemed inconsequential to actually having been a professional boxer at all. I realised that glory does not come in victory only and I was able to remember it all, the build-up, the run-down to a bout: always the same. Fighters fighting their boots onto their fee; fingers trembling to be clenched, not nimble enough for tying. Trainers' furtive faces looking upwards from bended knees and through knotted laces. Bandages unravelled and wrapped tightly around hands. Shorts and robes pulled on, towels everywhere.

Private box rooms and long communal corridor rooms in small halls where all the bill's boxers and managers and trainers are cooped and charged to change and fight. Finding yourself eyeing-up your opponent, looking at him almost guiltily, as you would a pretty girl, only with violence behind the eyes and not romance. A knock comes on the door from some unnamed underling whose job it is to keep pace with time, shouting, 'It's time!' His words release the slow tick of nervous terror that you thought was under control but that is uncontrollable, that parches the mouth and makes it impossible to relax.

Then the walk down a several cornered corridor and the boisterous noise of the half-drunk, fully intoxicated crowd increases in volume. The dissonance of several hundred or thousand whistles and cheers and human barks, contradicting and chaotic, emanating from below hundreds or thousands of eyes that you know are on you but that you can't see. All is light and noise. The cratered iron corner bucket stands full of liquefying ice and a blood stained sponge. Soft robes slip from tensed shoulders that undo themselves in shadowboxing; an introverted challenge, a war dance. The MC pulls you both in and repeats the mantra, the rules and regulations, the familiar stamp of officialdom. Four gloves come together, a square within a square, and touch in solidarity to those rules and to the unspoken spirit.

A lonely bell rings out above the tumult and brings the fighters together. Fresh fists slash the air in geometric jabs and hooks, and heads begin to buckle. Legs fall and rise, ropes bulge, blood flows, spectators wince, canvas burns and trainers feast on their own nervous hands. Athleticism reaches the apex of its peak, movement is synchronised, space is realised, devotion is redeemed and sacrifice yields. Strength of will, tenacity and the most deliberate and polished technique deliver an enormous left hook at the end of the seventh. Dreams are made real, egos erected, power is bestowed, prizes are piled high, glory is embraced and wealth is won.

Youth grows old, beauty is scarred, hope evaporates, plans fail, damaged veterans fight on because they know nothing else. Managers despair into the pit of their empty bank balance. The good, the bad, the talented. The boxers who were made for it and the ones who were made for anything but. The personalities, the grudges, the petty squabbles and the scrambling of the media-men. The unrecognisable faces, the broken noses, the swallowed teeth, the deep cuts and black eyes, the fractured jaws and the steady and secret destruction of minds.

And then a singing bell rings lonely above the tumult and it is all over.

Dear Sir,

I should like, through the medium of your paper, Boxing News, to announce to all my friends, my retirement from boxing.

May I thank you and your staff sincerely for always giving me just and fair reports and to all the people who have helped me in the fight game, a big thank you.

I shall always endeavour to help young lads who are interested in boxing.

To my trainer Nobby Wallace and Manager Mickey Duff, thanks for everything. I've had seven good years in pro. boxing and would advise any lad who had it in him to be a fighter to turn pro. It's a grand sport and I feel very sad to have to retire. But in all fairness to my wife and son and myself, my heart has gone from actual boxing.

Sincerely,

PAUL KING

THE BEST OF
THE REST

GERRY KING

Paul and Gerry King, May 1980

CHAPTER 28: THE BEST OF THE REST

I was born 27th October 1957, in St Thomas' Hospital, Lambeth, London at 7am weighing 7lbs, 7ozs. This momentous occasion was officially recorded on a short version birth certificate. The difference between a short and long certificate is detail. The short version just states name, date and place of birth, whereas the long certificate also records mother's maiden name and father's occupation. I have only ever possessed the short version, which I somehow managed to lose. As a result, in March 2012 I found myself on a 133 bus from Liverpool Street to Brixton, in order to obtain a replacement. At Lambeth Town Hall I filled in my details, paid the £9 fee and was told to come back in three hours, by which time the certificate would be processed. For some time I had been very preoccupied with the conclusion of this book and how much I could accurately remember of my dad's life after his boxing career. Being in this part of London with time to kill was a good opportunity to put some of my memories to the test.

When Dad married Mum in 1955 they were living at 1 Warriner Gardens, Battersea. In 1957 it was here that he would make the decision to retire from boxing, although there was a comeback fight after I was born. Dad's occupation on my birth certificate was recorded as 'steel fixer'. This job description was the first indication that he was distancing himself from boxing as a profession. It must have been a hard decision for him and I find it interesting he used this particular description, as he was a qualified refrigeration engineer. On reflection I think I can understand my dad's reasoning. He was working as a steel fixer with his brother-in-law, Harold when I was born and Mum and Dad's first child marked the beginning of significant change.

Within a couple of years we moved from Battersea and relocated seven miles away to Beverstone Road, Thornton Heath. In 1960 Thornton Heath would have been regarded as Greater London and a move out toward the sticks. Dad was now working for himself as a refrigeration engineer and had somehow secured a couple of garages full of Tedelex fridge spares. This had given him quite an edge as he was one of the few suppliers in London. It was in this house, whilst playing with my toy fort in front of the television, I heard that President Kennedy had been assassinated. I also have a memory of Mum mentioning Sabu the Elephant Boy had died. While we lived there my brother Ian was born, named after one of Dad's army pals, Ian George.

I caught a bus from Brixton, up past the broken façade of Streatham ice rink, to Thornton Health and wandered down Beverstone Road on the very pavement Dad taught me to ride my bicycle. The garages that stored his Tedelex spares were on Colliers Water Lane, which runs across the top of Beverstone Road. As soon as I saw the road sign it all came back to me. I remembered the market stall Dad had at Garrett Lane, Wandsworth, where he sold small fridges to landlords for bedsits. It was on the forecourt of a café; the owner's wife in the flat above had china-faced dolls all around the walls of her front room.

Later we moved fourteen miles from Thornton Heath to Easter Way, South Godstone; definitely Surrey and certainly the sticks. Near the Bluebell Railway and on the road to Brighton. I remember going from this address to Sir Winston Churchill's funeral and also my Nanny Lil, Mum's mother. Dad's refrigeration work continued and I recall sitting on his lap in his Bedford van, with the sliding door open. One day when we were going out in Dad's Vauxhall Estate the brakes failed and the front of the car went under the back of a lorry. Dad threw his left arm across myself and Ian to protect us. He seriously dislocated his shoulder; it was never the same again. There was no great compensation payout and as Dad was a self-employed sole trader, I'm sure this gave him the incentive to move us all to Devon and become a licensee in the town of his childhood.

We arrived in Torquay in a Pickford's removal van in 1966, the year of the England World Cup victory. The Crown and Sceptre was the first pub Mum and Dad managed. There was a massive room at the back and Dad converted this into a gym. Len Harvey came to stay and gave valuable publicity as well as Sammy Abbey from Ghana and the great Howard Winston from Wales. Dad became involved again in the local boxing scene and I remember us going to the Boxing Club. There was to be another pub after this, The Albert Inn, known as The Little House. I remember one of Dad's old boxing pals 'Honest' Joe Pring and his wife visiting from Bristol. Dad was not a success at running a pub and it was no doubt Mum's intuition that persuaded him to get out when he did.

Left to right: 'Honest' Joe Pring, his wife, Ian and Paul

In 1969 we moved again and ran a bed and breakfast during the summer months, while Dad had an assortment of jobs. I remember one particular job during the fuel crisis of the early 70s that involved coal yards. The deal was Dad would take orders for coal but the merchants had to physically offload the coal from, I think, German ships in various UK ports. We would sometimes go to Bristol and visit Joe Pring, as he was a coal merchant. He had a colour television and I remember watching *Jason and the Argonauts*. Dad always had a radio on the back parcel shelf of the car that we would listen to on these trips. I am still haunted by the Jimmy Young Show and the jingle: 'What's the Recipe Today Raymondo?'

The 70s did not start well. My dad's father died of a heart attack in New Zealand in 1970 and some months prior to this my mum had been seriously ill and was recovering from a cerebral haemorrhage. While she was in hospital Dad had bed and breakfast commitments to honour, as adverts had been placed in *Daltons Weekly*. We once served the gravy as soup and the soup as gravy; I don't think there was a return booking on that one. I always remember two girls from Sheffield who were great fun, telling me tales of their frolicks with the guys who ran the speed-boats on the beach.

Dad and I made many trips to London in the early 70s. We would go and stay with Charlie Hill, who was related to the 1950s 'King of the Underworld' Billy Hill. Charlie's wife Rose was a close friend of my Mum's. They had two fabulously sophisticated daughters and a son called Johnny who was the word in fashion. Uncle Charlie always had parrots and American cars; dealing in cars was one of his numbers. Later when Dad bought his Jag he was always supplied by Charlie when he needed exhaust boxes and part worn tyres. It was never boring going to see Charlie, even though I was often left in motors outside pubs with a bottle of coke and a bag of crisps. On one such occasion I remember nosing about in the glove box of a white Buick convertible and finding a load of watches. Going over to the Thomas à Becket on the Old Kent Road was always fun as I was allowed inside. I was told David Bowie had once used one of the upstairs rooms for rehearsals. It was the time of *The Sweeney* and armed robbery. Often Dad's inquiries concerning the whereabouts of old friends were met with prison release dates extending well into the future.

Dad stated working at the Carlton Club in Torquay in 1971. In December 1973 a gunman burst into the Carlton Casino. Dad's pal Paul Philby was on the Casino door and saw Marty Fenton coming toward him with a gun in his hand. Philby ran into the Casino and warned everyone that an armed man was coming up the stairs. There is no doubt that his warning saved lives, but in the ensuing madness three people were shot dead and a number wounded. I had worked part time for one of Marty's victims, Austin Webb, who was the manager of the Gibbons Bar and Restaurant on the Strand.

Marty had already shot dead a policeman on his way to the Casino. There was a connecting staff door from the Casino to the club next door and someone had run through to alert my dad. As Marty left the Casino, Dad came out of the adjoining club entrance; they faced each other on the street. Dad told me later: "He looked me straight in the eye but didn't say a word. He raised one of his guns. I don't remember feeling fear, just outrage. I wondered later why he hadn't shot me, until a copper told me he'd run out of bullets."

Marty Fenton owned the Virginia Hotel in Torquay and the company that had supplied much of the Carlton Club and Casino's fixtures and fittings. Marty was a serious drinker, womaniser and gambled to the point where it was a problem. His wife Patricia was a strikingly attractive dark-haired woman with a terrific sense of humour. Marty had become involved with some gamblers from the Casino and was losing quite a lot of money to them in private games at his hotel. It appears they were pressing Marty to get the money from John Tsigaridis the Greek Cypriot Casino owner. This would have been money for supplying fixtures and fittings and certainly outside any agreed business arrangements. Who knows? John was so secretive if you met him in a lift he wouldn't tell you if he was going up or down, but he was an astute businessman.

Marty's company was called Torbay Catering. I can remember the labels on the fridges, fryers and cookers in the Club kitchen. Historically there was no doubt Marty was an extremely intelligent guy as previous business successes had proved. However, this particular venture, coupled with his lack of self-control, was to be his downfall and have fatal implications for a number of people. In the subsequent court case one of the girl croupiers turned witness for the prosecution. She wanted to join the police force and had been assured her cooperation would ease her recruitment. Needless to say, when the case was over they dropped her like a hot brick. Apparently there had been incidents occurring in the Casino, petty dishonesty such as chips being knocked off the tables and palmed by staff; certainly not encouraged by the management. The tragedy is that the main players in this terrible sequence of events became the victims of degenerate individuals who got away with murder.

Earlier in 1973, prior to this deadly debacle, Dad had run off with Janet, a blonde nursing home proprietor from Scarborough, whom he had met in the club. I was to go into care while all this was happening and my younger brother Ian stayed with my mum. Dad went to live with Janet at Snips'; his old boxing pal and sports-writer for the local paper. This arrangement, in a confirmed bachelors home, removed any romantic notions and Janet eventually went back to her husband. Some time after this Dad visited me in the children's home, rather the worse for wear. He took me for tea in Buckfastleigh near Dartmoor in Devon and gave me a few quid. The Cat Stevens song 'Wild World' was playing on the eight-track in the car. I particularly remember this day because a housemaster called Hooper had attempted to stop my dad from taking me out. No one liked this guy. There was something intrinsically evil about him; ex services, shaved head, track suited. A bully. Dad warned Hooper in no uncertain terms what the consequences would be if I was prevented from going out with him. Years later, as an old man, Hooper was to be sentenced to seventeen years imprisonment, which is an indication of the gravity of his offences against young boys. I was fortunate, Hooper never gave me any problems and I am sure I owe that to my dad.

In the 1970s it was not unusual to see Ronnie Corbett, Anne Diamond or the 1950s singer Ruby Murray in the Carlton Club. Ruby was top of her game in 1955, she had five of her records in the British top 20 all at the same time. Both Ruby and my dad's stars had shone bright during the 50s; mutual success and an appreciation of the 'craic' fixed their friendship. Lenny Windsor, the local celebrity comedian who was to go on and play Las Vegas, would turn up regularly in his white Rolls Royce with the 4 LAF number plate. However, times changed and disco reached Torquay. The Carlton resisted, but eventually the restaurant closed, a DJ with an E type Jag replaced the band and the club was renamed Claire's.

The 70s were starting to fade and with it the glamour of the club. Dad realised it was time to move on. Back in the early 50s whilst on National Service, he had been encouraged in his boxing career and had qualified as a physical training instructor. It was this qualification and his experience that would provide his final source of income in a job he was terrific at and genuinely loved:teaching sport to the physically and mentally handicapped. Ironically, even though he worked for a hospital somehow his pay advice was printed on Devon and Cornwall Constabulary stationary.

Grand Charity Night

IN AID OF THE MENTALLY HANDICAPPED

*

Sponsored Boxing Tournament

Wednesday, 26th March

1980

at 7.30 p.m.

*

PALM COURT HOTEL
TORQUAY

*

ADMISSION PROGRAMME £1.50

CHAPTER 29: TWENTY 2-MINUTE ROUNDS

The Herald Express is a provincial newspaper covering predominately Torbay in Devon. In the late 1970s it was broadsheet. On the cover there used to be a late news section, running down the right hand side. If the paper was purchased at lunchtime from a vendor who hawked them round the harbour side pubs, this section was empty. It was here that my father Paul King and his drinking pals, mostly the unconventional self-employed, would make up their own news in biro. The main subjects were usually who wasn't paying their round, domestic disputes and nice little earners that involved copperised milk churns and 'original' prints framed from books. Sometimes world events inspired a mention. These creative writing classes would invariably occur in The Royal Vic, The Queens or The Hole in the Wall.

HUF 126E a gunmetal grey 4.2 Jaguar crouches at the curb while Paul King strikes a fighting pose outside 47 Warbro Road for the *Herald Express* photographer. You either put up or shut up. Stay cool and look mean. Hold that pose on the toes of an old pair of baseball boots; dark heavy cotton tracksuit bottoms with a few paint stains.

It's all about numbers. March 26th 1980, Paul King, The Torquay Tornado, will fight twenty 2-minute rounds in the ballroom of the magnificent seafront 'Queen of the English Riviera', Palm Court Hotel in Torquay. This boxing exhibition will hopefully raise five hundred pounds to purchase exercise equipment for the mentally and physically handicapped adults Paul works with at a local hospital. Attractive ringside bikinied girls are to announce the rounds on numbered boards and a cabaret will fracture the performance in a showbiz fashion. Jimmy Savile, the flamboyant bleach blonde, ex-wrestler, disc jockey, had been contacted as a possible contender. However, due to his own fund raising activities and Intercity train television filming schedule, he is unable to attend this spectacular event.

Paul King is forty-eight years old and enjoys a drink, cigars and a cavort. Paul believes that as long as he doesn't drink more than his doctor he's OK. His doctor, who has something of the Nigel Havers about him, is Peter Rovira; he also enjoys a drink and is a charmer. He will be in Paul's corner on fight night and right up until the end of his life. Paul has convinced Peter he will be fine, on the basis that 'Old Mongoose' aka Archie Moore, one time light heavyweight champion of the world, didn't retire from the ring until he was 47 years old.

Under the stairs of 47 Warbro Road, a terraced house a block away from Torquay United football ground, is a long khaki coloured canvas two-handled zip-up kit bag. Inside the bag is a pair of black leather-soled boxing boots with faded white laces. Wrapped in a pair of matching red Everlast shorts, gold monogrammed with the initials PK, is a fading-to-grey jock strap. On the back of a red silk dressing gown PAUL KING is embroidered in gold lettering and underneath TORQUAY. Years later, as a birthday present from my stepmother Paula, the dressing gown was to be mounted, framed and displayed in Paul's local pub in Torquay.

There is also a blue concertina toolbox. This holds small pipe cutters with hair lipped snouts, blunt and long-nosed pliers, coiled solder, black cloth tape and small screws pillowed in flux. Various refrigeration parts like thermostats, light switches and door seals all live under the stairs. One item belongs to my late mother Greta; a light blue Olivetti travelling typewriter with small white quick release square buttons either side of the handle. Greta had worked as a secretary for Morgan Crucible in London years before. When I think about it there was more about our family hidden away under the stairs, than on display in the front room. A sliding glass-fronted sideboard with a backlit cocktail cabinet contains Paul's bulky brown scrapbook, still welcoming snippets of his local escapades.

Twenty-two years from the barking MC's announcing seconds out; the glory days of the smoky halls and arenas, dancing on canvas, punch like a rivet gun. The nights of the club were behind him but there was time for one last escapade and Paul was never one to go gentle into that good night. He knew about the unlicensed fights in London but he'd never been part of a gang. He knew the score and this was his way to enter a final chapter of his life. It was all a bit of fun unless you wanted to make it something else. This was a significant time, half way between the start of his boxing career and the end of his life. On reflection, a truly noble mid-life crisis that did not involve Harley Davidson's, Thai brides or hair dye.

By March 1980 Mum was firmly in Dad's corner again.

 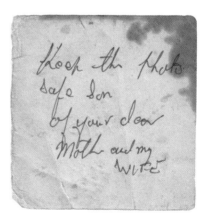

CHAPTER 30: EPILOGUE

Midday in early April 2008 finds me looking for a nursing home for my dad. I arrive unannounced at a double-entranced white villa in a beautiful part of Torquay. I later discover this palatial building has historical connections to Lillie Langtry. I meet the matron and four hours later I leave. Within a week my dad is living there, waking with a view across the bay.

Prior to this, Dad had been living alone for nearly eighteen months and not coping too well. My stepmother, Paula, had already gone into a nursing home. Dad told me Paula had burned out two clutches on the Ford Focus that he himself was to roll over a year later on his birthday. I thought Paula was different, there was young girl jollity about her, like a Tennessee Williams Southern Belle. I sent a spray of flowers to her from John Lewis for Christmas. I enclosed a card and told her I loved her and that she had been like a mother to me. I thanked her for her kindness as she had always bought me warm clothes as birthday and Christmas presents. Paula never received the spray or the card as she was admitted to a nursing home a week before Christmas. Dad thought she would come home but she never did, and their little nest fell apart from December 2006 onwards.

I remember their home as always welcoming, bright and spotless. Paula always took great pride in the little touches, like the small bouquet of silk flowers in a fluted wall vase above the telephone table. I remember the glass curio cabinet filled with small treasures and keepsakes from foreign holidays, the extending table and chairs with padded lime-green ribbed seats, the comfortable three-piece floral suite corralling a long glass coffee table. On the coffee table, alongside a cut-glass bowl filled with liquorice allsorts, was a wooden cigar box carved with a boxing glove and my dad's name. On the walls were his prints and pictures and photos of Paula's nieces.

I would occasionally stay in the snug spare room with mirror-fronted wardrobes, filled with boxing memorabilia. I'd read myself to sleep, usually with books by old boxers, self-published, signed by the authors with a dedication to my dad. I remember I would often take Paula and Dad a cup of tea in the morning, placing the cups on their matching bedside cabinets. The Jarman and Platt bedroom suite was cream with gold trimmings; the wardrobe had little porcelain panels painted with flowers.

After Paula died I'd go and visit Dad, clean up and cook a meal, but everything was falling apart. Here was a man not used to looking after himself, drinking too much and smoking too many cigars. A chip-pan fire, a bad leg getting worse, spillages, domestic appliances breaking down; Dad broke down and went into hospital. Time had taken its toll. I would tell Dad that Mick Jagger was still performing and there was only fourteen years between them. Dad would reply that Mick Jagger hadn't had his life. I learnt the differences between residential and nursing care, and the funding implications. My perception of time changed. It wasn't the filmic flipping calendars with numbers and dates blowing away to oscillating strings. I made time brutal; violent in its intent. This was not the fault of time, of course it was I who had taken time for granted. One day Dad said to me: "I dreamt I could run again, fast and easy. Then I woke up and felt my stiff, useless knee." He looked at me wide-eyed and resigned, then he smiled and said, "I like the flying dreams. At least when I wake up I know where I stand."

I would take Dad out in my old black diesel Saab. He would be hoisted from his wheelchair on to the covered front seat and we would motor up to an exclusive area with stunning views of the South Devon coastline, where, as Dad would always remind me, Max Bygraves had lived. Looking out over the bay, huge oil tankers were playing for time, waiting for prices to go up or weather to calm down. I would always make Dad a bottle of brandy and water, a plastic one with a pop-up stopper. Sometimes he couldn't get a tight grip so I'd give the bottle a good squeeze, which he appreciated. We had stopped using glasses as he kept dropping them and my car was beginning to smell like a pub. I especially remember blustery winter days when we would sit listening to a Roy Orbison and Cat Power CD compilation. Dad particularly liked the track 'Lived in Bars' by Cat Power. I noticed on the cover of her CD 'The Greatest', a pair of gold boxing gloves hang from a gold chain. Dad would lift his right hand, cigar between his fingers, and like Johnny Shannon in the Nic Roeg film Performance, he'd say "I like that son, turn it up." It wasn't so much the words of the song, it was the sentiment we both shared.

Those billowing, rain-lashed days reminded me of the weather in south Wales and walking in the Black Mountains with an artist called Roger Cecil. Roger was more than ten years younger than my dad but I remember his resilience and determination, and I wanted some of it for Dad. I wanted him to walk again. But that was never going to happen.

Dad's cigar would go out and he'd ask me to light it. I'd take the sodden cigar from him and feel like a bad son and a selfish bastard for resenting his spittle. Some situations I was never sure how to handle, such as Dad asking me to help him get his cock into a urine bottle. I always checked his stoma bag before we went out and made sure his nails were kept clean and cut. I could never have imagined that these things would happen. But life goes on until one day it calls time. I knew that Dad wasn't going to resist going 'gently into that good night' this time. He wasn't raging against anything any more. I could sense his tiredness and that's why we would sit quietly together, letting nothing stressful into our orbit. I assured him he had nothing to worry about, that everything was OK and all was well.

I had been at my dad's bedside with his sister Edna, my auntie, for over four days. She had flown into Heathrow on one of the last planes from the States before the volcanic ash hit. Time took on a routine, rotational pace; resting, reading, handholding, brow-wiping, lip moistening, looking at photograph albums. Edna and I would exchanges stories and there were revelations for both of us. We both realised it was just a matter of time. There was not going to be any miraculous recovery, this was the end. I fetched fragrant candles, flowers and odour neutralizers to mask the smell of death in the room.

My dad passed away at 4.45 a.m. on Wednesday 21st April 2010. I showered and changed my clothes, putting on a pair of his casual trousers that had his room number written with indelible ink on an inside pocket. Edna and I talked, cried and laughed; then it was time for her to go. Dust cloud restrictions were lifted and she flew out on one of the first planes to the States the following day.It was a beautiful sunny morning as he was shushed away from the bright white Victorian villa. In a long black car, he passed through silent streets with occasional palm trees, to the undertaker's premises that had been his local newsagents years before. I remember my mum had always bought the *Daily Mirror* there and I would get my *NME*. Later on, I went to the under-taker's to sort out arrangements. On the way, I met Paul the Continental Hairdresser who was out getting his newspaper. I told him Dad had passed away that morning and he let out a string of expletives, running his hand through his magnificent bouffant grey hair.

Weeks later I was reading an article about an artist who had created a piece of work using clips from films that, either in the script or the image, referred to a specific time. This twenty-four hour film in real time is potentially endless. The artist had mentioned that the lead-up to midnight was intense, whereas the hardest time to cinematically fix was 5 a.m. I thought about all the unconventional hours I had spent in my dad's company.

In the early 1970s when Dad worked at The Carlton, I would help the chef in the kitchen, making up prawn cocktails and Melba toast. The chef and I would watch the cabaret from behind the glass-fronted cooler counter fridge. A resident band provided the backing music for various singers and entertainers, including a belly dancer and numerous comedians. I remember a couple called Steve and Bonnie who played guitar and sang. Steve had long blonde hair and Bonnie was black with a superb Afro. The Carlton Club hours were 8 p.m. till 2 a.m. Some nights, after closing time, I would go with Dad to eat late meals at Greek restaurants or to parties on the beach or in rented bungalows in Paignton. Bow ties skew-whiff, fighting poses with pals, banter such as "Careful, I'm delicate." Driving home along the seafront, a beautiful railway poster morning, the sun hot on the vinyl seats of the Ford Corsair, the 'Walrus of Love': Barrence Eugene Carter, playing on the eight-track.

Years later, on Sunday mornings, still half-cut from the night before, we would park up, waiting for the 12 o'clock pub opening, listening to Derek and Clive, the irrational alcoholic laughter, tears running down our faces, father and son in a scene a southern Shane Meadows has yet to capture. Over the limit, over-emotional, yet knowing that time was significant.

When the time came, I dipped my finger into the powder that was once Dad and scattered his ashes at a spot where we had always parked and looked out over the bay, listening to music. Barry White to Chan Marshall. The endearments, the threats, the empty promises and well-intentioned grandiosity are now just words on a page. I have thought about my dad a great deal since he passed away in April 2010. Sometimes these thoughts are sentimental, but sometimes I selfishly search for clues as to my character. I wonder how well I knew my dad. I believe the last three years of his life were the years when we were closest. I took a renewed interest in his glory days and shared his memories. I wanted to understand him more and make sense of the past and celebrate it in my future. I know he had regrets about my mother, Greta; he told me this. He often asked me if he had been a good father. I always said yes.

In June 2010 the memorial service was held for Dad in St Mathias Church, Torquay, within sight of the school he had attended as a child. The Vicar Gordon Ripley was an excellent showman and started the service with: "Seconds out round one". There were many old friends: Paul the Continental Hairdresser, Ian Baker, Jill, Richard and Veronica together with much loved family. His sister Edna dedicated a poem and his granddaughter Alexi lit a candle in his memory. The ex-boxers who shared a camaraderie with my dad, stood together like a guard of honour. These proud men caused me to remember boxing reunions I had attended with Dad and how gentle they always were considering the nature of their sport. For me they will always be true tough guys. From the local boxing fraternity it was wonderful to see Gordon White, Kurt Ernst, Dave Stacey and the artistic Peter Hayfield. The record that concluded the service was Barry White singing 'Let the Music Play'. I had bought this record for Dad in 1974, on the occasion of his 43rd birthday. He'd always loved it.

Paul King, 2009

GLOSSARY OF BOXING TERMS

WEIGHTS

LIGHT FLYWEIGHT
The lightest weight a boxer can be. The weight limit for light flyweight in professional boxing is 108 pounds (49 kg)

FLYWEIGHT
A weight in boxing and other sports inbetween light flyweight and bantamweight
In boxing it ranges from 108 to 112 pounds (48-51 kg)

BANTAMWEIGHT
A weight in boxing and other sports in-between flyweight and featherweight
Professional boxer weighing 112-118 pounds (51-53.5 kg)
Amateur boxer weighing 112-119 pounds (51-54 kg)

FEATHERWEIGHT
Professional boxer weighing 118-126 pounds (53.5-57 kg)
Amateur boxer weighing 119-126 pounds (54-57 kg)

LIGHTWEIGHT
Professional boxer weighing 130-135 pounds (59-61 kg)
Amateur boxer weighing 126-132 pounds (57-60 kg)

LIGHT WELTERWEIGHT
Inbetween Lightweight and Welterweight
In professional boxing a limit of 140 pounds (63.5 kg)
In amateur boxing up to 141 pounds (64 kg)

WELTERWEIGHT
Inbetween lightweight and middleweight
Professional boxer weighing 140-147 pounds (63.5-66.5 kg)
Amateur boxer weighing 140-148 pounds (63.5-67 kg)

MIDDLEWEIGHT
Professional boxer weighing 154-160 pounds (70-72.5 kg)
Amateur boxer weighing 157-165 pounds (71-75 kg)

LIGHT HEAVYWEIGHT
Professional boxer weighing 160-175 pounds (72.5-79.5 kg)
Amateur boxer weighing 165-179 pounds (75-81 kg)

HEAVYWEIGHT
Professional boxer weighing more than 175 pound (79 kg)
Amateur boxer weighing 178-200 pounds (81-91 kg)

SUPERWEIGHT
Only in amateur boxing.
Amateur boxer weighing more than 200 pounds (91 kg)

CATCHWEIGHT
A weight mutually agreed upon by two boxers, when boxers of different weight classes meet in the middle

---

0-10
10 POINT MUST SYSTEM
In the 10 Point Must System of scoring a fight the winner of a round must receive 10 points. The loser of a round will receive from 9 to 6 points
A close round: 10-9. One knockdown: 10-8. Two knockdowns: 10-7
Three knockdowns: 10-6. No knockdown but one fighter completely dominates round: 10-8. Can't pick a winner: 10-10

A GEE
A showman boxer, to excite the crowd for effect

BOLO PUNCH
A flashy wide sweeping uppercut that is more for show than power. The bolo punch might not even be used at all but rather used to distract the opponent so you can hit them with your other hand

BOUT
A match that consists of rounds with a one minute break

BOXING BOOTHS
Until the 1960s funfairs included boxing in their entertainment and had boxing booths in which matches took place. This went into decline in 1947 after the British Boxing Board of Control prohibited these matches

BRAWLER
A slow and lazy fighter, whose movements are predictable

BREADBASKET
The stomach

BUM RUSH
A way of rushing an opponent to get them out of the fight quickly

CANDY CANE
A punch used by Sugar Ray Robinson, thrown with a right hand to the body slightly turning it over and pushing downward

CATCHER
A catcher uses his head to block his opponent's punches

CHIN
To have the ability to stay on your feet even after getting hit by a very powerful punch

CLINCH
When one boxer holds onto the other to avoid being hit

COUNTERPUNCH
A counterpuncher waits for his opponent to throw a punch, blocks or slips past them and then exploits the opening in the opponent's position with a counter attack or punch

CROSS
A power punch thrown with a boxer's dominant hand

DIRTY FIGHTING
Holding an opponent's head down and hitting repeatedly in ribs, or throat. Stepping on the opponent's foot and punching, head butting and making it appear accidental

FALL THROUGH THE ROPES
When a boxer falls through the ropes, they are given a 20 count to get back up and cannot be assisted

FLASH KNOCKDOWN
When a no-count occurs; a boxer is knocked down but gets back up before the referee starts counting

GATE
The total amount of money that a fight brings in from the people who have attended it

GLASS CHIN
Glass chin or glass jaw refers to boxers who are knocked out easily

HAWKERS
Businessmen or traders who travel and act as an agent in a commercial transaction

HAYMAKER
A swinging punch thrown with all of the person's weight behind it. Term first appeared in 1912, perhaps referring to "hitting the hay" going to sleep

INSIDE FIGHTER
An inside fighter gets very close to their opponent and hits them with a series of punches, overwhelming them

JOURNEYMAN
A good boxer who strives to be successful yet still has some limitations and has no expectations of winning a match. They are often hired to fight up and coming boxers to add something to their experience

LACING
Using the laces on the boxing gloves to rub and cut your opponents face

LIVER PUNCH
A short quick punch to the liver with a left hook. It's one of the most effective punches in boxing and guaranteed to bring your opponent down; it is sickening as well as paralysing

MAJORITY DECISION (MD)
When two of the three judges score one boxer as the winner, while the third judge scores neither boxer a winner (a draw)

MAJORITY DRAW

When two judges vote for a draw, while the third judge chooses a winner. The fight is recorded as a draw on both boxers' records

MANDATORY EIGHT COUNT

An 8-second count that a fallen boxer must wait for after he gets back up. It gives the referee time to decide whether the boxer can continue the fight or not

MEMORIAL TEN COUNT

When a bell is rung ten times at the beginning of a fight in honour of a recently deceased boxer

MOONLIGHTERS

Boxers who act as substitutes

MOUSE

Swelling of the head, forehead or face

NEUTRAL CORNER

One of the corners of the boxing ring not assigned to any of the boxers. After a boxer has been knocked down the opponent has to stand in the neutral corner while the referee does the count

NO DECISION (ND)

If a fight is booked for more than four rounds and an accidental foul occurs that causes a severe injury, the referee has to stop the fight and the fight will result in a 'No Decision' if stopped before the four rounds are complete

NOBBINS

British slang for money thrown into a boxing ring by the crowd in appreciation of a good contest

NOT BEING ABLE TO GET OFF
A fighter struggling to get started and throw successful punches

ON THE BUTTON
To be punched on the bottom of the chin

OUTSIDE FIGHTER
A fighter who tries to maintain the gap between himself and his opponent by fighting with longer punches

PALOOKA
A palooka is a poor boxer with no talent who usually loses his fights in four or six rounds to boxers who are just starting their careers. There was a comic strip in 1928 by Ham Fisher that featured a kind but slow-witted boxer called Joe Palooka

SPIELER
An announcer or showman

UNDERCARD
The event or events coming before and supporting the main boxing match

Also published by Lubin Publishing

"The absurdism of a Lear or a Lewis Carroll refracted through the noir novels of Derek Raymond. Great stuff." – **WILL SELF**

Lubin Tales
GERRY KING

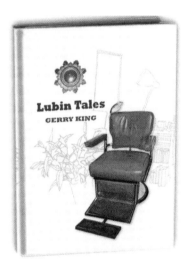

LUBIN TALES is a 64-page hardback, pocket-sized collection of beautifully illustrated short stories – a debut collection of short stories and musings by artist and performer Gerry King.

Surreal, playful and romantic, the stories are woven together from various locations and time frames; an abandoned 1947 V-12 Lincoln automobile waits for a history in a French wood, British seaside resorts are portrayed with renewed love and nostalgia. A host of characters tease and entertain; the fabulous Pauls, one a continental hairdresser, the other a 1950s welter-weight boxer, plus the promenade-prancing Poodle Faker and the deliciously deviant Stealerant.

Each page is a visual delight, colour throughout with graphic illustration and photography.

DESIGNED AND
ILLUSTRATED
BY LOUISE BURSTON

ISBN: 978-0-9563077-0-5
Retail Price: £10.00
Binding: Hardback
Illustrations: Colour and B&W
64 pages, 162mm x 114mm

LUBIN PUBLISHING
www.zerolubin.org
zerolubin.wordpress.com

LIMITED EDITION LETTERPRESS PRINTS

'NOBBINS' (above) and 'PERFORMANCE'
210gsm handmade paper 400mm x 760mm 2 x colour
Every print signed and numbered by artist Ben Goodman for Zero Lubin
Available direct from the publisher www.zerolubin.org
£47.00 each including post and packing.